New Directions in Hospitality and Tourism

Annual review of hospitality and tourism trends

Edited by Richard Teare and John T. Bowen

MCB
University Press

CASSELL
London and Washington

Cassell
Wellington House,   PO Box 605
125 Strand   Herndon
London WC2R 0BB   VA 20172

First published 1997
British Library Cataloguing-in-Publication Data
A catalogue record for this book is available from the British Library.

ISBN 0 304 70141 6

Typeset by Richard Teare
Printed by Redwood Books, Trowbridge, Wiltshire

Other Titles in the Hospitality and Tourism Resource-Based Series:

Series Editor: Professor Richard Teare

- Strategic Management
- Marketing Management
- Operational Techniques
- Operations Management
- Management Skills
- Consumer Marketing
- Small Business Management
- Leisure and Tourism Operations
- Management in Leisure and Tourism

New Directions in
Hospitality and Tourism

Contents

Abstracts & keywords

Trends in the UK hotel industry
BDO Hospitality Consulting, UK

Keywords Economic conditions, Hotels, Tourism, United Kingdom

Reviews UK hotel sector performance during 1995 with reference to prevailing economic conditions and political prospects. Considers the likely impact of changes in employment policy and European directives, general trends in the UK and reviews the hotel market in London and the English regions, Scotland and Wales.

Hospitality and tourism impacts: an industry perspective
Jorge Costa and Gavin Eccles

Keywords European Union, Hospitality industry, Reports, Tourism, Trade associations

Reviews the activities of the European Union (EU) (1994-95) and the published work of UK-based associations, government bodies, analysts and consultants (1990-95). Identifies the relative influence of the EU in gaining wider recognition for hospitality and tourism and industry research in tracking salary trends and the performance of hospitality firms among others.

Organizational trend analysis of the hospitality industry: preparing for change
Shane C. Blum

Keywords Catering industry, Hospitality industry, Human resource management, Service quality, Strategic management

Examines aspects of change as reflected by articles published in the *Hospitality Research Journal* during the seven-year period from 1989-1995. Discusses how change (demographic, technological, societal, legal, cultural or ethical) is likely to influence the industry in relation to six themes: human resource management, service quality, hospitality education, the food service sector, strategic management and legislation. Summarizes sub-themes and observations with reference to the likely impact of change on the industry in the medium term.

Diverse developments in travel and tourism marketing: a thematic approach
Clark Hu

Keywords Economics, Market segmentation, Psychology, Strategic marketing, Tourism

Reviews developments in travel and tourism marketing as reflected by articles published in the *Journal of Travel and Tourism Marketing* over a four-year period from the journal's inception in 1992-1995. Identifies five main themes (economic psychology, market segmentation and travel patterns, strategic marketing, technological advances and travel and tourism communications) and related subthemes that portray a pattern of diverse research and development relating to the practice of travel and tourism marketing.

Perspectives on tourism development
Gavin Eccles and Jorge Costa

Keywords Airlines, Planning, Sustainable development, Tourism, Transport, Trends

Examines aspects of tourism development as reflected by articles published in: *Annals of Tourism Research, Tourism Management* and *Travel and Tourism Analyst* during 1995 (sustainable tourism, transport, new products and the future of tourism) and during the six-year period from 1989-1994 (social trends in tourism, tourism planning and the airline industry).

Challenges for hospitality and tourism operators: a North American perspective
Sridhar Prabhu

Keywords Hospitality industry, Human resource development, Marketing, Operations management, Tourism

Identifies five main themes from the articles published in the *Cornell Hotel and Restaurant Administration Quarterly* during a five-year review period from 1990-1995. The theme areas (hospitality training and education, human resources and organizations, restaurant and food service operations, hotel operations and development and travel and tourism management) serve to identify some of the main challenges that hospitality and tourism operators are currently facing.

Hospitality operations: patterns in management, service improvement and business performance
Richard Teare

Keywords Company performance, Hospitality industry, Improvement, Operations management, Service quality, Strategy

Provides an overview of developments in hospitality operations management as reflected by articles published in: *International Journal of Contemporary Hospitality Management, International Journal of Hospitality Management, International Journal of Service Industry Management* and *Service Industries Journal* during 1995 (business performance, customers and service improvement, operations and the curriculum, strategy and development) and during the six-year period 1989-1994 (structural relationships in hospitality and tourism, operations and business development, strategy and systems development, human resource development and quality improvements).

Managing environmental change: insights from researchers and practitioners
John T. Bowen

Keywords Catering industry, Hospitality industry, Strategy, Technological change, Tourism, Trends

Analyses the articles published in the *FIU Hospitality Review* during a seven-year period from 1989-1995. Identifies seven main themes: people and organizations; marketing; environmental change; total quality management and strategy; education; financial analysis and accounting practice; tourism and technology. Summarizes by highlighting the linkages between the themes and the related sub-themes.

Clusters and gaps in hospitality and tourism academic research
Hadyn Ingram

Keywords Hospitality industry, Information technology, Management, Service quality, Tourism

Content-analyses the academic entries in the WHATT-CD International Hospitality and Tourism Research Register using four broad categories – general management issues hospitality, tourism, and current or "hot" research issues. Identifies clusters of research interest within these categories and identifies "gaps" in the form of relatively unexplored research topic areas.

Editorial

Welcome to the "Second annual review of hospitality and tourism trends" which aims to provide a concise overview and commentary on the themes portrayed in the literature, by academic research and by the wide range of reports emanating from industry, analysts, consulting firms, trade and professional associations and government organizations. To accomplish this, our key task is to construct strands of research and thinking by drawing on the many hundreds of articles and reports published between 1989-1995. To begin, we targeted a group of respected European and North American-based academic journals and so to some extent the picture we provide is bounded by the positioning and style of each journal. Additionally this year, we have sought to reflect the views of associations, government and industry by drawing on a variety of UK and European Union related publications and we aim to extend the industry perspective in next year's Review.

The 1996 Review includes an overview of hotel industry trends in the UK, provided by Review sponsors BDO Hospitality Consulting, and eight articles that reflect the ongoing data-gathering work of the research teams based in the UK and North America. To encourage integration and cross-comparison, these articles provide summary tables and thematic relationship diagrams so as to highlight the emerging themes as clearly as possible. In this respect, the review articles fulfil several functions; they provide a reasonably detailed commentary and at the same time, provide a conceptually-based summary for readers who are more interested in the broader thematic relationships. Readers who would like to attend a series of one-day seminars on hospitality and tourism trends are invited to contact the HCIMA on e-mail: library@hcima.org.uk for further information. Four UK seminars are currently planned for the week of 24-30 March 1997, hosted by Forte Hotels.

In 1997, the Review will provide a wider international perspective by reporting on developments in the Asia Pacific region with a commentary provided by the research team based at Southern Cross University, New South Wales, Australia, directed by Nerilee Hing. Together, the three teams maintain the HCIMA's Worldwide Hospitality and Tourism Trends CD-ROM (WHATT-CD) project with specific responsibility for two of the three WHATT-CD databases; the *International*

Hospitality and Tourism Research Register and *World Trends* database.

Our longer-term goal is to facilitate a continuous discussion on international developments in hospitality and tourism and to help to shape a collective vision of the future. A means of achieving this is provided by the Hospitality & Tourism Forum on the Internet at URL: http://www.mcb.co.uk/services/hospitality_forum/home.htm where readers will find a virtual academy series in hospitality and tourism, Internet conferencing and other resources for practitioners and academics. The Forum offers a global meeting point on the Internet to enable managers, academics and students to share and communicate ideas and information. We hope that the Annual Review will help to stimulate Forum debate by providing a self-contained resource and an accompanying guide for WHATT-CD users in industry and education. If your organization has a World Wide Web site and you'd like to join the Forum, please contact Andrea West on e-mail A.West@surrey.ac.uk for more information.

We wish to express our sincere thanks to the organizations and their representatives who have provided generous sponsorship and support for the 1996 Annual Review. In alphabetical order they are: BDO Hospitality Consulting (Jonathan Langston, Liz Prescott, Trevor Ward); Cassell plc (Noami Roth and her team); Forte Hotels (Patrick Copeland, Keith Wainwright); Granada Group plc (Stephanie Monk); HCIMA (Rosemary Morrison, David Wood) and MCB University Press (Jonathan Barker, Gordon Wills). Finally, thank you to Brenda Kitson, Pauline Taylor and the MCB University Press production team for the quality of their ongoing work, which is much appreciated.

Richard Teare
Research Director (Europe),
Worldwide Hospitality & Tourism Trends
John T. Bowen
Research Director (North America),
Worldwide Hospitality & Tourism Trends

Worldwide Hospitality & Tourism Trends: an HCIMA project with research centres in Europe (University of Surrey) North America (University of Nevada, Las Vegas) and Australia (Southern Cross University). The Annual Review is published by MCB University Press and by Cassell plc (London and New York) with sponsor support.

MCB University Press
Awards for Excellence
Outstanding Paper

The publisher and Editor of the
International Journal of Contemporary Hospitality Management
are delighted to announce that

Jackie Brander Brown
Manchester Metropolitan University, UK
and
Brenda McDonnell
Sheffield Hallam University, UK

are the recipients of the journal's 1996 Outstanding Paper
Award for Excellence

Their paper, "The balanced scorecard – short-term guest or long-term resident?", which appeared in Volume 7 Numbers 2/3 was chosen by the Editor and Editorial Advisory Board as best meeting the editorial and readership objectives of the journal, taking into account content and excellence of presentation.

"Highly Commended"

"Menu design: can menus sell?"
John T. Bowen and Anne J. Morris
IJCHM, Volume 7 Number 4

"Managing complexity for competitive advantage:
an IT perspective"
Elaine Crichton and David Edgar
IJCHM, Volume 7 Numbers 2/3

"Marketing strategies for fast food restaurants:
a customer view"
Ali Kara, Erdener Kaynak and Orsay Kucukemiroglu
IJCHM Volume 7 Number 4

**The awards will be presented at a ceremony to be held
on 11 March 1997**

LITERATI
· C L U B ·

Trends in the UK hotel industry

BDO Hospitality Consulting, London, UK

Reviews UK hotel sector performance during 1995 with reference to prevailing economic conditions and political prospects. Considers the likely impact of changes in employment policy and European directives, general trends in the UK and reviews the hotel market in London and the English regions, Scotland and Wales.

Introduction

After some pretty grim times in the early 1990s, when hotel profits and values dropped simultaneously, the hotel industry reports some very welcome news for 1995, with operating results much improved on the previous year, and with confidence of continued growth at an all-time high. While the experts disagree on the level of growth in the economy as a whole, there is no dispute that the recession is behind us, and that things are getting better. But economic stability – especially evidenced by sustainably low inflation and interest rates – is not matched by political stability. Within the next 12 months, we will have a general election, and there is a real chance of a change of government at that time, if today's opinion polls are to be believed. There is a great deal of uncertainty about Labour's policies in many areas, but one thing is clear – wage costs will rise.

The Labour Party has made the introduction of a minimum wage the central plank of its employment policy. The Labour leadership has not, as yet, set out the rate for a minimum wage but at their party conference in October 1995, the trade unions, supported by a number of delegates in the hall, were strong in their call for the figure to be set at £4.15 per hour. Clearly the introduction of a minimum wage at this level will have severe and damaging repercussions in the tourism industry.

The hotel and catering industry relies heavily on part-time and casual staff, together with flexibility of hours and overtime. Inevitably jobs will have to be restructured and that means fewer. Even at £4.15 per hour, research estimates 950,000 jobs could be lost across Britain and full restoration of pay differentials could take the figure to 1.8 million. We expect that a huge slice of job losses would fall in the tourism industry.

It is not just impending national changes which cast clouds on an otherwise bright picture in the UK's hotel industry. We have seen from the current "British beef" crisis how decisions taken in Brussels can affect British industry and British jobs overnight. So hoteliers should be aware of the potential effects of the Social Chapter, effects that they have so far avoided due to the opt-out secured by the present government. The Labour Party supports the Social Chapter on the basis that a well motivated and secure workforce increases productivity and competitiveness, and no-one can deny that they have the best of intentions.

Employment legislation under European Social Policy promises to unleash wide-ranging laws on employment. The Working Time Directive, challenged by the British Government, sets out restrictions on the number of hours people can work – 48 hours in a week, no more than 13 hours a day, eight hours on night work and four weeks paid holiday. Not only does this restrict overtime for the zealous but also impinges on flexibility, so vital to hoteliers. While some of this legislation is laudable in its intent, policymakers, and those bidding for national power, must not work in a theoretical model, devoid of practical knowledge and application. Hotels are a 24-hour business, and policies and legislation which could do lasting damage to our great and successful industry should be resisted strongly.

Having introduced some of the main trends affecting the UK's hotel industry, we will now analyse some of these aspects in more detail. For this purpose, we divided the country in several different geographic regions, namely London, Provinces, Scotland and Wales, which will be analysed in terms of the main aspects affecting this industry. Before moving to the analysis of the regions a general overview of the UK's situation is now provided.

General trends in the UK

Since sterling's exit from the European Exchange Rate Mechanism (ERM) in 1992, the economy in the UK has continued to show steady rates of growth, and optimism over the short to medium term remains relatively high. The weakening of the pound against currencies in some of the key demand-generating markets contributed to significant increases in the number of tourists visiting the UK in 1995. The total number of overseas tourist arrivals reached a record figure of 23.6 million, representing a 12 per cent increase

BDO Hospitality
Consulting, UK
*Trends in the UK hotel
industry*

over 1994, while revenue from overseas tourists amounted to £11.7 billion, an 18 per cent increase over the previous year. The British Tourist Authority (BTA) forecasts a further increase to 25.2 million visitors for 1996, with revenue expected to increase to £12.8 billion.

Tourism growth has been accompanied by increased government commitment to the industry as a key component of the economy. Contributing £33 billion or 5 per cent of Gross Domestic Product (GDP), tourism now earns more for the UK than North Sea oil or the financial services sector. The Department of National Heritage's benchmarking review of the smaller hotel sector, *Competing with the Best*, has recently been published, while improvements continue to the English Tourist Board's (ETB) Crown Accommodation Classification and Grading Scheme. Further initiatives include more effective and targeted marketing by both the BTA and ETB, a review of the way in which the tourism industry uses its human resources and efforts to create a cross-party approach to tourism among Ministers in parliament.

Nevertheless, continuing economic growth in 1995 has had a positive impact on business confidence in the UK. Coupled with increases in business and leisure tourism, the hotel industry has experienced further increases in average occupancy and achieved average room rates over 1994. Furthermore, many hotel companies reported an increase in profits. Mount Charlotte reported a 50 per cent rise in pre-tax profits for 1995 to £35.5 million, while operating profits for the Savoy Group rose by 155 per cent to £12 million, with a 10.6 per cent increase in achieved room rate over 1994. The smaller hotel groups also performed well, one of the best performances in the sector in 1995 being that of Arcadian International, with a share-price rise of 35 per cent.

Investment activity was dominated by the high profile and controversial £3.9 billion take-over of Forte by Granada, which eventually went ahead in January of this year, some months after the initial bid had been placed in the Autumn of 1995. Granada's acquisition of Forte's assets, from its Posthouse, Heritage and Travelodge properties to the Exclusive hotels in London such as the Grosvenor House, Hyde Park and Browns, and its international hotels, in addition to Forte's 68 per cent shareholding in the Savoy Group, has thus resulted in a wealth of bid enquiries as Granada proceeds to discuss the disposal of former Forte assets with potential purchasers. However, the company appears to be in no hurry to conclude a deal.

Other major group ownership changes in 1995 were the purchase of Copthorne Hotels from Aer Lingus by CDL Hotels International of Singapore, and Whitbread's acquisition of Scott's Hotels, the UK Marriott Franchise. Furthermore, many of the world's major hotel companies are expanding their activities in the UK and a number of high profile mergers and/or acquisitions have occurred or are the subject of current rumours.

London

London continues to be at the forefront of the UK's tourism industry, accounting for over 50 per cent of all overseas visits. In 1995, London received 21.3 million visitors, of which 12.5 million were from overseas, representing a 16.8 per cent increase over 1994. Domestic visitors to London increased by 17.3 per cent in 1995 to 8.8 million, from 7.5 million the previous year. Overseas visitor spend amounted to almost £6 billion in 1995 and the London Tourist Board (LTB) forecasts a further increase for 1996 to £6.5 billion. Expenditure by domestic tourists was £1.16 billion in 1995. The LTB also expects total visitor numbers to London to increase by 3 per cent in 1996 to 21.9 million. The majority of this growth is expected to come from overseas, with the domestic market remaining constant. Increases in tourism activity in London enabled the optimism experienced by hoteliers during 1994 to be further enhanced last year. These developments are reflected in the improved average occupancy and average room rates reported in this year's UK Hotel Industry survey.

The hotel market in London, now considerably stronger than in any other major European city, has benefited from an increasingly competitive UK economy and the weakness of the pound relative to some currencies in the main demand-generating economies. In addition, continuing supply constraints, coupled with the lack of prime development space, have further enhanced occupancy rates and achieved average room rates. The buoyancy of the sector during 1995 can be illustrated by a high level of expansion and takeover activity as many of the world's major hotel companies or organizations looked to capitalize on London's status by selling their hotel assets at a profit and/or by investing in a growth market.

High profile ownership and management changes in London during 1995 included the sale of The Ritz by Trafalgar House to the Barclay brothers (signalling Trafalgar House's withdrawal from the hotel sector after almost 20 years), while Thailand's

Landmark group added The Regent to their portfolio. The Royal Garden, Kensington, was sold by the Rank Organisation to the Goodwood Group of Singapore, and Prince Al-Waleed Bin Talal of Saudi Arabia acquired the Four Seasons Hotel.

Take-over activity in London has been complemented by a number of expansionary and refurbishment developments at many hotels. The Royal Garden Hotel is due to reopen in 1996 subsequent to its acquisition by the Goodwood Group and a £28 million refurbishment programme, while refurbishment also began at CDL's Gloucester, Chelsea and Bailey's hotels. The Savoy, The Berkeley and Claridge's are also undergoing substantial refurbishment programmes. At the Charing Cross Hotel, 83 luxury twin and double rooms were created, with additional suite development also at the Hotel InterContinental and the Royal Horseguards Hotel. Related projects include a new conference venue at Whitehall Place which opened in 1996, in addition to expansion at the London Commonwealth Institute and a new conference centre adjoining the Gloucester Hotel.

Continued interest in hotel properties in London, by both domestic and international investors, indicates that the outlook for 1996 and beyond remains very positive. A number of luxury hotels, including the Langham Hilton and the Britannia InterContinental, have changed hands at premium prices, and some developers are looking to convert disused office space to hotels in order to overcome supply constraints. London Docklands is continuing to develop as a prime commercial and residential centre and could attract further hotel development as transport links and image improve. Greenwich also has the potential to attract development, having won the bid to stage the Millennium Exhibition, with plans to develop the site subsequently into a leisure complex, while the success of the Novotel at Waterloo may stimulate further hotel development south of the river, an area which has been otherwise largely ignored by the hotel industry in London. Other future developments include Whitbread's plans for the former Greater London Council building, and also the development of additional Travel inns in central London, for example at Putney Bridge. The former Londonderry Hotel in Park Lane is due to reopen in June 1997 as the Metropolitan Hotel.

Provinces

Provincial hotels also reported increased room occupancy and average room rate results during 1995. Steady economic growth in the UK coupled with competitive labour costs, interest rates and low inflation, was reflected in increased business confidence and growth in the volumes of domestic and international tourism. The stability of the UK economy, in relation to high-cost and less productive economies in other Western European countries, has attracted investment from South-East Asian and Far Eastern nations such as Japan and South Korea.

The hot weather during summer 1995, coupled with exchange rates which make popular destinations such as France more expensive for British holidaymakers, encouraged UK residents to make more use of the tourist facilities on offer at home, benefiting, in particular, traditional British seaside resorts. Favourable exchange rates also made Britain a cheaper holiday option for many overseas visitors. Despite these positive developments, the accommodation sector in the Provinces still feels that much untapped potential remains, especially in the domestic market. The increasing availability of, and lower costs of travel to, previously expensive or remote holiday destinations, resulted in the majority of tourism expenditure by UK residents being remitted abroad. Further, the percentage of people staying in hotels as opposed to visiting friends and relatives or self-catering accommodation, remains relatively low.

Overall, the business and conference market continued to be a buoyant sector for hotels in the provinces during 1995, while economic growth and increasing levels of disposable income have helped to stimulate the weekend leisure market. However, hotels are still having to be fiercely competitive in terms of rates and value for money in order to attract further demand from this sector.

As with the London hotel market, the provinces witnessed a significant amount of ownership management changes and other developments during 1995. The Granada takeover of Forte stimulated renewed interest in Britain's budget sector properties and in the motorway lodge market, particularly with regard to Granada's take-over of Pavilion Services, while both the Regal Hotel Group and Macdonald Hotels (recently floated on the Stock Exchange) strengthened their portfolios with the acquisition of additional properties. Stakis, the Scottish hotel group, acquired the Carlton Manor in Corby and the Palace Court in Bournemouth, and CDL's purchase of Copthorne Hotels included six properties in the Provinces. Other acquisitions included Principal Hotels' purchase of the Chesford Grange hotel in Kenilworth from the receivers of Periquito Hotels, the sale of the

Cheltenham Park Hotel to Paramount Hotels, Arcadian International's purchase from the receivers of Woodlands Park in Cobham, Surrey, and Whitbread's acquisition of the UK Marriott franchise. New openings included Slaley Hall in Hexham, the Cheltenham/Gloucester Moat House, and the Palace Hotel, Manchester, by Principal Hotels.

Scotland

As with the UK in general, the tourism industry in Scotland, worth £2 billion per year and contributing 5 per cent of GDP, continues to be a key component of the Scottish economy. The Scottish Tourist Board (STB) expects a 12 per cent increase in visitor numbers in 1995 to 11.6 million compared with 10.3 million in 1994. In 1995, spending by UK visitors in Scotland was estimated to have increased by 10 per cent over 1994 to £1.4 billion, while the number of trips increased by 14 per cent to 8.9 million for the period January to November 1995. Expenditure by overseas tourists during 1995 was expected to have increased by 9 per cent over 1994 to £865 million. Scotland's market share of all tourism expenditure in the UK also increased in 1995, rising to an estimated 10.3 per cent from 9 per cent for UK residents, and to an estimated 7.9 per cent, from 7.7 per cent, for overseas tourists. Visitor numbers were boosted by, among other factors, the success of feature films such as Rob Roy and Braveheart.

The buoyancy of the hotel market in Scotland led to an increase in hotel buying and selling activity, particularly towards the end of 1995. In July 1995, the Bank of Scotland sold its entire portfolio of 30 hotels to Trevor Hemmings, the leisure director of brewer Scottish & Newcastle. Macdonald Hotels were brought in to manage the properties. Thistle Hotels continued their refurbishment programme, including Glasgow's Hospitality Inn & Convention Centre which has been upgraded and rebranded as the Glasgow Thistle Hotel. New openings in 1995 included the 134-room Stakis Edinburgh Airport Hotel.

The hotel industry in Scotland benefited particularly from the opening in September 1995 of the £38 million Edinburgh International Conference Centre, which is expected to attract over 100,000 business visitors a year. The conference market is buoyant in Scotland, with Edinburgh second only to London in popularity as a conference city. Extension and redevelopment of the Scottish Exhibition and Conference Centre (SECC) in Glasgow, in time for the 25,000 delegate World Rotary

Congress in 1996, should have further positive impact on the hotel sector.

In Aberdeen, the accommodation sector benefited from the development of new leisure facilities at Aberdeen Beach. The completion of a new hotel in the area this year in addition to the construction of other leisure facilities, should further contribute to the revitalization of the city in terms of its ability to attract overnight visitors. Other related developments in the Scottish provinces in 1995 included the purchase of the Aviemore Ski Centre and resort by Premier Land. Other high profile projects in Scotland include a deluxe hotel in Glasgow which is being redeveloped from the former Sheriff Court, and Glasgow-based Stakis continue their acquisition strategy with property purchases in Scotland and England.

Wales

Wales continues to be a popular tourist destination, particularly among English visitors and in 1995 the Wales Tourist Board (WTB) estimated that approximately 8.5 million visitors came to Wales from England. This represents an increase of 27 per cent over 1994. Overseas visitors were estimated at 700,000, an increase of 100,000 over 1994.

The WTB expects the number of visitors to Wales to reach 10 million by 2000, and there has been particularly strong growth in two-way tourist traffic from Ireland, especially to Anglesey. Marketing initiatives have been established to increase the scope of facilities and attractions that are on offer to tourists to Wales. For example, in an effort to make aspects of Wales' heavy industrial past more attractive to tourists, some areas have been turned into industrial museums, while the "Great Little Railways of Wales" have also been developed. Harbours such as Porthmadog and Plas Menai have been transformed to offer a range of watersports, and the gold-mining area of Dolgellau is now a popular tourist attraction. In October 1995, the Welsh Development Agency established a Network Wales service on the Internet, providing information on business issues, tourism, finance and property. In addition, travel agents from the USA were invited on familiarization trips to increase awareness of Wales among American tourists.

The major ownership change in Wales in 1995 was the sale of the Cardiff International Hotel by Brent Walker to Jury's Hotel Group for £7 million. CDL's acquisition of Copthorne Hotels included the Copthorne Cardiff, while Granada's takeover of Forte also had an impact in Wales, including properties in Cardiff, Swansea and elsewhere.

Thanks to improving economic conditions in the UK as a whole and increased levels of tourism activity both to and within the country, the outlook for hoteliers in Wales appears to be positive. Although the oil spill at Milford Haven caused concerns that the local tourism industry would suffer, these concerns were only short-lived, and the area was fully restored before the main tourist season began.

Conclusion

From the review of the main events in the UK's hospitality industry some particular trends clearly emerge. After some hard times in the early 1990s, with hotel profits and values dropping simultaneously, the hotel industry showed definite signs of recovery in 1995, with operating results improving on the previous year. Despite experts' disagreement on the level of growth in the economy as a whole, there is no doubt about the stage of recovery that we are going through at the moment. In terms of other important aspects to bear in mind concerning the future of the UK's hotel industry, the following can be put forward:

- the General Election, and the chance of a change of government;
- the possible introduction of a minimum wage and its repercussions in the tourism industry;
- the EU Working Time Directive with its restrictions on the number of hours people can work;
- the expansion of many of the world's major hotel companies in the UK and the possible occurrence of further high profile mergers and/or acquisitions;
- the expected increase of total visitors to London;
- the continued interest in hotel properties in London by both domestic and international investors.

The improving economic conditions in the UK in general and the increase in the levels of tourism activity provides a positive perspective for hoteliers. However, it is important that they take into account the main trends occurring in their business environment and use these to review their goals and strategies. This should be done on a regular basis so that managers can ensure that plans and actions are integrated into a dynamic business strategy.

Further reading
United Kingdom Hotel Industry, BDO Hospitality Consulting, London, 1996.

Hospitality and tourism impacts: an industry perspective

Jorge Costa
Research Manager (Europe) Worldwide Hospitality and Tourism Trends,
Department of Management Studies, University of Surrey, UK
Gavin Eccles
Research Manager (Europe) Worldwide Hospitality and Tourism Trends,
Department of Management Studies, University of Surrey, UK

Reviews the activities of the European Union (EU) (1994-95) and the published work of UK-based associations, government bodies, analysts and consultants (1990-95). Identifies the relative influence of the EU in gaining wider recognition for hospitality and tourism and industry research in tracking salary trends and the performance of hospitality firms among others.

Introduction

This article reviews the hospitality and tourism themes and their related sub-themes as reflected in the publications of the European Union, trade, industry, professional bodies and organizations. The themes are analysed through both tabular and written descriptions and a thematic diagram is given.

The publications are analysed under three main headings covering different periods of analysis:

1 European Union action 1994-1995.
2 Associations 1990-1995, hospitality associations, tourism associations.
3 Industry 1990-1995.

European Union action 1994-1995

In considering the actions taken by the European Union (EU), one can note 18 different cases with the potential to affect the hospitality and tourism industry (see Tables I and II for details). The first major concern for the industry is the imposition of VAT (value added tax) on tour and travel packages in March 1994[1]. The impact of this action is likely to be a rise in the cost of holidays, as all trips sold will carry a 15 per cent common travel VAT rate. The European Tour Operators Association has requested European Members of Parliament to table questions about future levels of VAT on travel packages, in the hope that the commission may look again at this regime. Within the same month, the European parliament concluded that it had failed in its attempt to gain wider political recognition for tourism[2]. If entrance status had been secured, then many firms would have been entitled to industry grants. The general feeling within tourism seems to be that insufficient political pressure was brought on the commission to bring tourism into the list of priorities for future programmes and funds.

During April/May 1994 two relevant actions concerned with pre-payments of bookings made by telephone or letter were debated in the EU[3,4]. This ban has been a matter of concern among hotel and tour operators in the UK. The background to this ban is the commission's preliminary aim of protecting consumers against fraudulent mail order. In essence the aim of the directive was to provide guarantees for consumers, but its effect would have been to put small hotels and tour operators out of business. The proposals were stalled in the council and the Greek presidency drew up a compromise text which dropped the ban on pre-payments. A consensus was therefore agreed whereby services with reservations should be exempt from the article. Further actions were discussed that will effect the tourism industry. First, the commission proposed the details of cases where import duties are waived on the transportation of goods from one member state to another[5]. This action is of great importance for cross-channel ferry operators, as well as airport retail shops. Second, the commission drew up plans to help small businesses trading and operating across European borders[6]. As the industry comprises many small businesses, this legislation may play a greater part in the success of these firms in the years to come.

One of the most prominent actions undertaken by the EU during 1994, which will affect hotels, is the employment of third country nationals[7]. The consensus here is that admitting third country nationals for employment purposes will from 1 January 1996 be 'the exception rather than the norm". In future, admission of third country nationals for employment will only be allowed when vacancies cannot be filled by national and community manpower. This action will be of significance to hotels with its high level of temporary, seasonal and non-national workforce. Finally, the commission published a guide to clarify the loans and grants available, which happened after reports in trade journals indicated that EC money was available for the industry[8].

One of the most relevant EU actions in 1995 was the Commission's tourism action programme[13]. Here the commission produced a proposal for the greater collection of statistical data, to be achieved by employing greater numbers of staff to do the work. Second, the commission issued a consultative document

[**11**]

Jorge Costa
and Gavin Eccles
*Hospitality and tourism
impacts: an industry
perspective*

Table I
European Union action 1994

EU action	Focus	Sub-theme
VAT on tour and travel packages[1]	The European tour operators association requested a motion on the future of VAT on travel packages	Tourism and the impact of VAT
Failure of the European year of tourism[2]	The failure in attempting to qualify companies for industrial grants	Industrial recognition
Distance selling directive[3]	To ban the pre-payments of bookings made by telephone or letter	Problems for small hotels
Distance selling directive[4]	Exclusion of the ban on pre-payments from the directive, and the creation of a new proposal to protect the consumer against fraudulent mail order	Opposing the pre-payment ban
Duty free[5]	Commission's proposal with details whereby import duties are waived on the transport of goods from one member state to another	Ferries and airport shops
Small and medium-sized enterprises[6]	To help the climate for small businesses trading and operating across European borders	Use of the tax system to assist small business
Employment of non-EU nationals[7]	Admission of third country nationals for employment	Temporary and seasonal staff
European funds[8]	Commission's guide to clarify the loans and grants available from the EU	Development loans
Community measures affecting tourism[9]	The first commission report to consider all fields of the tourism industry, from statistics to education	Tourism industry
Hotels and safety[10]	European parliamentary commission proposal for a directive on fire safety in hotels	New legislation
Timeshare properties[11]	Directive to introduce EU-wide protection for purchasers of timeshare property rights	Tourism goodwill
Job creation and investment[12]	World travel and tourism council report on job creation and investment in the tourism industry	Potential job creation

asking for comments from organizations involved in tourism, which could then be used to help generate new ideas[14]. This document would also enable the commission to produce a list of all organizations in member states responsible for tourism.

Following previous work on small businesses in hospitality and tourism[8], the commission produced a document on payment periods in commercial transactions[15]. This recommendation is a response to calls for legislation enforcing prompt payment for goods and services between companies, as well as across borders. This should help those businesses that are having to wait long periods for payments from customers in other European countries.

Associations 1990-1995

Hospitality associations

In reviewing reports conducted by hospitality associations during the period 1990-1995, it can be noted that two particular associations have contributed much work to the industry, the Hotel and Catering International Management Association (HCIMA) and the British Hospitality Association (BHA) (see Table III). During 1990, both the HCIMA and the BHA commissioned reports to look at salaries and benefits and to provide an analysis of salary trends for use by both members and non-members[19,20]. The relevance of reviewing salaries is that it can help determine an actual picture of pay and any benefit

Jorge Costa
and Gavin Eccles
*Hospitality and tourism
impacts: an industry
perspective*

Table II
European Union action 1995

EU action	Focus	Sub-theme
Action plan for tourism[13]	Commission's proposal for the collection of field data and determination of future budgets	Statistical data
European Union in the field of tourism[14]	Consultative document asking for comments from firms involved in tourism	Options for the future
Small businesses[15]	A recommendation on payment periods in commercial transactions, and legislation enforcing prompt payment for goods and services	Payment of bills on time
Rural tourism[16]	Initiative report on the future of rural tourism by EU member states local government representatives	Tourism in Europe
Overbooking of hotels[17]	European commission asking hotel companies to participate in a study to look at the problems of overbooking	EU concern for service quality
Fire safety in hotels[18]	Commission's result of their tender for a contract to assess fire safety in hotels	Security issues

Table III
Hospitality associations' reports 1990-1995

Association's report	Focus	Sub-theme
Hotel and Catering International Management Association (HCIMA) – salaries and benefits in the hotel industry[19]	To dispel the impression of low pay and low status and to promote a more positive image of the industry	Changes in salary structure
British Hospitality Association – wages and salaries in hotels[20]	How changes in the economy can play a major part in company pay and benefits	Salaries and the economy
British Hospitality Association – wages and salaries in hotels[21]	Trading conditions and how they have resulted in mixed fortunes for employee wage levels and managerial salaries	The use of more part-time staff
HCIMA – European management skills in the hospitality industry[22]	The identification of knowledge and skills requirements in the initial stages of a manager's career	Continuing professional development
HCIMA – pay and benefits in the hospitality industry[23]	The abolition of wages councils and how the hospitality industry will now enter a new era regarding pay and remuneration packages	Employee expectations
British Hospitality Association – contract catering survey[24]	The contract catering industry in the UK and how its 75,000 employees serve 500 million meals a year with an annual turnover approaching £1 billion	Career and job opportunities
British Hospitality Association – minimum wage proposals[25]	The introduction of a minimum wage and how such policy may affect the hospitality industry	The response of the industry
British Hospitality Association – contract catering survey[26]	A review of contract catering activities: from education to military contracts	Emergence of new markets
British Hospitality Association – contract catering industry[27]	The growth of new areas: a notable trend within contract catering	Market expansion

Jorge Costa
and Gavin Eccles
*Hospitality and tourism
impacts: an industry
perspective*

progressions for employees. These surveys can dispel the impression of low pay and low status and help promote a more positive image of the industry. Both reports, though, note very slow movements in salary levels during these recessionary times.

In the issue of wages and salaries, the BHA noted that 1991 would be a transitional year for pay scales within the industry[21]. The recessionary pressures of the first year of the 1990s became further ingrained in 1991, with cutbacks in both corporate and individual spending. This report also showed a changing attitude among employers, looking for improvements in staff efficiency in response to the harsh trading environment. One major hotel group decided to convert a number of full-time contracts into part-time contracts in order to retain flexibility of staff deployment in slack trading periods. The BHA find this indicative of the industry tendency to increase the use of part-time staff. It seems probable therefore that an increasing number of lower-skilled jobs will need to be offered to more mature employees, who are looking already for part-time positions.

In order to review the operational aspects of the industry, the HCIMA commissioned a report to identify skills requirement in the initial stages of a manager's career[22]. This focused on the needs of managers as they climb the success ladder, and whether they should abandon their traditional "craft-based" approach. In conclusion the HCIMA note a need to develop and stretch managers throughout their career, providing a stimulus for fulfilling the "middle years".

To conclude the analysis of the reports by hospitality associations it is interesting to look at the report produced by the HCIMA in 1993 where councils will be abolished[23]. The implications seem to enable the hospitality industry to enter a new era with regard to pay, where employers are now in the same position as those in most other industries have always been. In fact, from now on they are entirely responsible for setting their own levels of remuneration.

Tourism associations
The majority of the work conducted within tourism is commissioned by the British Tourist Authority (BTA), with the help of the English Tourist Board (ETB). From this work several important themes can be identified (see Table IV). Starting by looking back to 1990, the BTA[28] announced that travel and tourism is the largest industry in the world in terms of employment and ranks in the top two or three industries in almost every country of the world. This particular year broke all records in terms of tourist arrivals and

receipts, and further analysis of the international tourist arrival statistics shows that holiday travel accounts for 60 per cent of world arrivals. These large number of tourists also account for about 5 per cent of all global sales. One year later, figures show that international tourists made 425 million trips, an increase of 2.6 per cent on the previous year[29]. The BTA also looked at the overseas visitors to the UK, where in the first two months of 1991 overseas residents made 1.8 million visits to Britain, a fall of 18 per cent compared with the same months in 1990. It must be noted that the Gulf war which started in the middle of January and did not end until the end of February affected the flow of international travelling throughout the world. In looking at 1992, one can also record many international events which affected the flow of international tourists[30]. The US presidential election as well as the UK's departure from the exchange rate mechanism created uncertainty not only within the business community but also among consumers.

As the economies of the western world began to pull free from recession, so the number of tourists was seen to be increasing. The BTA[31] noted that 13.1 million overseas visitors came to Britain in 1993, an increase of 3 per cent compared with the previous year. The study of overseas visitors to London provides a detailed picture of the behaviour of visitors to the capital, and can be used further to enhance the products on offer[32]. The major implication from this report is that trade/exhibition visitors spend more per visit than both the average tourist and the average business visitor. Finally, 60 per cent of all tourists visiting London were EC residents.

Looking at a different subject, the Tourism Society reports on the teaching of tourism courses[33]. In its London conference, May 1992, tourism education was a focus of widespread debate, where the aim was to identify the major issues and inform and widen debate among educationalists, employers and policy makers. The main focus was defining the appropriate roles of education and developing links between education and industry. Employers are not totally aware of what tourism courses offer, and judge their future employee intake on general intellectual abilities and previous experience.

From 1993 the BTA note that the British tourism industry seems to have turned the corner[34]. Overseas visitors to Britain passed the 20 million mark and occupancy in English hotels returned towards the levels last seen in the late 1980s. Taking bed-nights as a measure of volume, it is noted that we are likely to have seen at best zero growth in the

Jorge Costa
and Gavin Eccles
*Hospitality and tourism
impacts: an industry
perspective*

Table IV
Tourism associatons' reports 1990-1995

Associations' report	Focus	Sub-theme
British Tourist Authority (BTA) and English Tourist Board (ETB) – tourism intelligence quarterly[28]	The year of 1989 in terms of arrivals and receipts	Impact of tourism
BTA/ETB Economic research – tourism intelligence quarterly[29]	International tourists' trips in 1991: an increase of 2.6 per cent on the previous year	UK tourism
BTA/ETB Economic research – tourism intelligence quarterly[30]	The effects of tourism on the British economy: tourism's share of GDP and tourism as a proportion of all exports	Tourism indicators
BTA/ETB Economic research – tourism intelligence quarterly[31]	Overseas visitors in 1993 and a comparison with the same period in the previous year	Tourism trends
BTA/ETB Statistical research – overseas trade fair/exhibition visitors to the UK[32]	Trade fair and exhibition visitors and their spending per visit: how it compares with the average visitor and the average business visitor	Business tourism
Tourism Society – what are we teaching tomorrow's professionals[33]	Identification of major issues in tourism education: the debate among educationalists, employees and policy makers	Education and industry
English Tourist Board – the state of the market[34]	Overseas visitors to Britain in 1995	UK tourism growth
BTA/ETB – Statistical research – overseas visitors to London survey[35]	Overseas visitors to London	Tourist behaviour
Scottish Tourist Board – Scottish tourism strategic plan[36]	How Scotland can receive a greater number of tourists: a requirement to promote the landscape, culture and people	Tourism planning
English Tourist Board – the state of the market[37]	The main holiday market and its changes in two decades: 1975 to 1994	New tourism initiatives
Wales Tourist Board – a strategy for Wales[38]	The need for tourism to be continually developed owing to its substantial contribution to the economy	Tourism planning
English Tourist Board – English heritage monitor[39]	The continual monitoring of conservation, presentation and public use of England's architectural heritage	Tourism and conservation

British domestic market over the five-year period 1990-1994, but by the same measure and over the same five years, Britons' tourism abroad has grown by one third. Suggestions that the UK recession of the early 1990s would benefit the domestic, at the expense of the outbound, market appear to have been ill-founded. In looking to the future, the BTA highlight the twin issues of "bookability" and "price transparency" as critical areas for attention. In looking at bookability, the high street travel agency is the dynamic interface for holiday tourism. Through the retail sector, operators are able to let the consumer see much more of the product on offer and help to facilitate the ease of purchase. Therefore we should not be surprised that an independent, often family-run, unbranded hotel or guest house finds it difficult to compete with large operators.

Industry 1990-1995

In reviewing the industry through the work of consultants (see Table V) we start with the work of Pannell Kerr Forster (PKF). In a report published in 1990, PKF note that hotel

Jorge Costa
and Gavin Eccles
*Hospitality and tourism
impacts: an industry
perspective*

Table V
Industrial reports 1990-1995

Industrial report	Focus	Sub-theme
Pannell Kerr Forster – hotel product segmentation in Europe[40]	To determine which conditions encourage product segmentation within France, Germany and the UK	Branding
Pannell Kerr Forster – corporate hotel users in the UK[41]	Today's corporate hotel user and his critical views on products that do not come up to the growing expectations	Business travellers
Kleinwort Benson Securities – quoted hotel companies[42]	Hotel price earnings ratio and hotel demand	Economic cycles
Kleinwort Benson Securities – quoted hotel companies[43]	The growth of companies with hotel exposure on continental Europe and how it compares to that of companies constrained within the UK	Market development
Kleinwort Benson Securities – quoted hotel companies[44]	The performance of hotel companies and how this will be determined more by competitive strategies than overall improvement in the markets	Strategic hospitality management
Pannell Kerr Forster – outlook UK Trends[45]	The improvement of occupancy levels before price increases and/or reduced discounting can take effect	Occupancy and pricing
Kleinwort Benson Securities – quoted hotel companies[46]	Firms with international exposure and how they generate half of their hotel profits through foreign operations	Internationalization
Hotel and Catering Training Company – meeting competence needs[47]	The employment rise in the hospitality industry up to the end of the century	Human resources
Kleinwort Benson Securities – quoted hotel companies[48]	Bad performance of hotel shares and prospects for recovery	Competitive environment
Pannell Kerr Forster – outlook UK trends[49]	The UK hotel market and its improvement in demand levels	Rising occupancy levels
Pannell Kerr Forster – outlook UK Trends[50]	Improvements in hotel performance and continued growth in occupancy	Performance and investment

companies in Europe need to be familiar with influences at work in the US hotel market, in particular market segmentation[40]. In looking at Germany, France and the UK, the three largest hotel markets in Europe, PKF conclude that a greater requirement for branding is required, as this approach has enabled US firms to establish an international presence across the globe. The idea of the brand should enable products constantly to fulfil expectations, as people staying within the hotel knows exactly what they will get during their stay. During 1991, PKF conducted research into corporate hotel users in the UK[41], where they concluded that today's businessperson is well travelled and can be very critical of a product that does not come up to growing expectations.

The years 1990 and 1991 witnessed harsh times for hospitality and tourism, owing to the Gulf War and recession. In the 1991 report[42], Kleinwort Benson set out to

persuade institutions that by the end of 1991 funds should have moved to a 15 per cent growth position in the hotel and leisure sector. The basis of their argument is that shares have been undervalued and that hospitality companies should see strong earnings recovery as the next economic cycle emerges. Their report in 1992 has similar positions to those from the previous year. Here they note that only large hotel chains will perform better than small hotel chains, and that companies with hotel exposure in continental Europe will provide greater medium to long-term growth than those constrained in the UK[43].

In considering 1994, Kleinwort Benson, in their world quoted hotel companies report, argue that the hotel market grew substantially in 1993, and expected the performance of hotel companies to be determined more by competitive strategies rather than overall improvements in markets[44]. In turn, PKF reviewed the situation in the UK[45] and

Jorge Costa
and Gavin Eccles
*Hospitality and tourism
impacts: an industry
perspective*

came to the conclusion that in recent years this market has been dominated by consolidation and gradual profit recovery. Room occupancy levels have improved by an average of 6.2 per cent, although average rates continued to soften. This is a classic post-recession recovery scenario, as it is necessary to rebuild volume before price increases and/or reduced discounting can take effect.

Finally, looking to 1995 Kleinwort Benson note that hotels have entered a trend of developing more effective supply and improving operating practices[46]. The general supply trend is that companies are selling obsolete hotels, whilst new developments are targeted at more efficient budget lodges. It looks like the larger companies are performing materially better than smaller chains, and it seems that the tendency is for this trend to remain as an industry norm.

Conclusion

In reviewing the main trends identified in the publications under analysis during the period from 1990 to 1995, the following concluding observations can be put forward:

• The imposition of VAT (value added tax) on tour and travel packages in March 1994 and the consequent rise in the cost of holidays, as all trips sold will carry a 15 per cent common travel VAT rate. The EU made a failed attempt to bring tourism into the category of an industry, which, had it been successful, would have entitled many firms to industry grants. Also important was the action on the employment of third country nationals. This means that in future, admission of third country nationals for employment will only be allowed when vacancies cannot be filled by national and community manpower. This action will be of significance to hotels with its high level of temporary, seasonal and non-national workforce.

• The industry tendency to increase the use of part-time staff, with a major hotel group already converting a number of full-time contracts into part-time contracts, in order to retain flexibility of staff deployment in slack trading periods. Another interesting change is that of the wages councils being abolished. As a result, employers are now in the same position as those in most other industries, where they are entirely responsible for setting their own levels of remuneration. This event brings about a situation where the industry can become self-regulating with regard to pay.

• The study of overseas visitors to London showed that trade/exhibition visitors

spend more per visit than both the average tourist and the average business visitor, and also that 60 per cent of all tourists visiting London are EC residents. Another important issue is that concerning tourism education. This has been the focus of widespread debate among educationalists, employers and policy makers. A report by the Tourism Society focused on defining the appropriate roles of education and the links between education and industry. In this report it is possible to see that employers are not totally aware of what tourism courses offer, and judge their future employee intake on general intellectual abilities and previous experience.

• Hotel companies in Europe need to be familiar with influences at work in the US hotel market, in particular market segmentation, as this approach has enabled US firms to establish an international presence across the globe. In terms of performance, the trend is for hotel companies to be now determined more by competitive strategies rather than overall improvements in markets. Finally, hotels need to develop a more effective supply and also improve their operating practices.

Figure 1 (which appears after the Reference list) provides a summary of the main themes and sub-themes and of the proposed actions to face the trends occurring.

References
1 "VAT on tour and travel packages", written question, E-0708/94, March 1994.
2 "Failure of European year of tourism", *EP Report,* A3-0069/94, March 1994.
3 "Distance selling directive", European Business Link, London, April 1994.
4 "Distance selling directive", *COM(93),* final - SYN 411, May 1994.
5 "Duty free", *COM(94),* 232, July 1994.
6 "Small and medium sized enterprises", *Official Journal,* C 187, 9 July, 1994.
7 "Employment of third country nationals", European Business Link, London, August 1994.
8 "European funds", European Business Link, London, August 1994.
9 "First report from commission on community measures affecting tourism", *COM(94),* 74, April 1994.
10 "Hotel safety", *Parliament Report,* A3-310/94/A, May 1994.
11 "Timeshare", *EP Report and Resolution,* C4-0133/94, September 1994.
12 "Job creation and investment in the tourism industry", *Copy of WTTC Report,* October 1994.
13 "Tourism action plan", *COM(94),* 582 final, 14 January 1995.
14 "European Union in the field of tourism", European Business Link, London, April 1995.

Jorge Costa
and Gavin Eccles
*Hospitality and tourism
impacts: an industry
perspective*

15 "Small businesses", *Official Journal*, L127, 10 June 1995.

16 "Rural tourism", *Committee of the Regions Opinion*, CdR/19/95, March 1995.

17 "Over-booking of hotels", *Official Journal*, C84, 6 April 1995.

18 "Fire safety in hotels", *Official Journal*, C252, 28 September 1995.

19 *Salaries and Benefits in the Hotel and Catering Industry*, Hotel and Catering International Management Association, London, 1990.

20 *Wages and Salaries in Hotels*, British Hospitality Association, London, 1990.

21 *Wages and Salaries in Hotels*, British Hospitality Association, London, 1991.

22 *European Management Skills in the Hospitality Industry*, Hotel and Catering International Management Association, London, 1992.

23 *Pay and Benefits in the Hospitality Industry*, Hotel and Catering International Management Association, London, 1993.

24 *Contract Catering Survey*, British Hospitality Association, London, 1991.

25 *Minimum Wage Proposals*, British Hospitality Association, London, 1992.

26 *Contract Catering Survey*, British Hospitality Association, London, 1992.

27 *Contract Catering Survey*, British Hospitality Association, London, 1995.

28 *Tourism Intelligence Quarterly*, Vol. 11 No. 3, BTA/ETB Economic Research, January 1990.

29 *Tourism Intelligence Quarterly*, Vol. 12 No. 4, BTA/ETB Economic Research, April 1991.

30 *Tourism Intelligence Quarterly*, Vol. 14 No. 2, BTA/ETB Economic Research, November 1992.

31 *Tourism Intelligence Quarterly*, Vol. 15 No. 2, BTA/ETB Economic Research, November 1993.

32 *Overseas Trade Fair/Exhibition Visitors to the UK*, BTA/ETB Statistical Research, 1993.

33 "What are we teaching tomorrow's professionals, Tourism Society Conference, London, May 1992.

34 *The State of the Market*, English Tourist Board, January 1995.

35 *Overseas Visitors to London Survey*, BTA/ETB Statistical Research, 1994.

36 *Scottish Tourism – Strategic Plan*, Scottish Tourist Board, 1994.

37 *The State of the Market*, English Tourist Board, July 1994.

38 *Tourism 2000 – A Strategy for Wales*, Wales Tourist Board, 1995.

39 *English Heritage Monitor*, English Tourist Board, 1995.

40 *Hotel Product Segmentation in Europe*, Pannell Kerr Forster Associates, London, 1990.

41 *Corporate Hotel Users in the UK*, Pannell Kerr Forster Associates, London, 1991.

42 *Quoted Hotel Companies*, Kleinwort Benson Securities, London, 1991.

43 *Quoted Hotel Companies*, Kleinwort Benson Securities, London, 1992.

44 *Quoted Hotel Companies*, Kleinwort Benson Securities, London, 1994.

45 *Outlook UK Trends*, Pannell Kerr Forster Associates, London, 1994.

Jorge Costa
and Gavin Eccles
*Hospitality and tourism
impacts: an industry
perspective*

Figure 1

1990-1995 – summary of main themes and subthemes and actions proposed to face trends

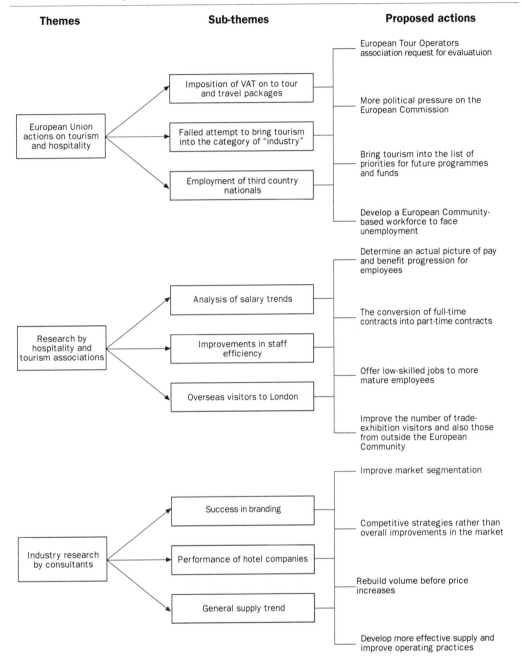

Organizational trend analysis of the hospitality industry: preparing for change

Shane C. Blum

Research Manager (North America) Worldwide Hospitality and Tourism Trends, William F. Harrah College of Hotel Administration, University of Nevada, Las Vegas, USA

Examines aspects of change as reflected by articles published in the *Hospitality Research Journal* during the seven-year period from 1989-1995. Discusses how change (demographic, technological, societal, legal, cultural or ethical) is likely to influence the industry in relation to six themes: human resource management, service quality, hospitality education, the food service sector, strategic management and legislation. Summarizes sub-themes and observations with reference to the likely impact of change on the industry in the medium term.

Introduction

The purpose of this review is to examine the emerging themes relating to the 135 articles published in the *Hospitality Research Journal* (HRJ) from 1989 to 1995. The six main themes identified are:

1 people and organizations;
2 service quality and customers;
3 education and training;
4 finance, strategies, and performance;
5 trends analysis, food service sector;
6 legal considerations.

Each theme is subsequently divided into sub-themes, and the overall focus of the *Hospitality Research Journal* over this period can be ascertained by viewing the accompanying tables associated with each main theme.

Theme 1: people and organizations

Effective human resource management has become a vital component for creating and maintaining a competitive edge in today's hospitality industry. Table I summarizes the human resource sub-themes, beginning with Goll's[1] "Management by values" which stresses a consistency between the values of the organization and the individual in order to help create a positive organizational environment.

Employee empowerment and leader-member exchange (LMX) are two common "buzzwords" in the field of human resource management. Sparrowe[3] examines the likely effects of organizational culture and LMX on empowerment. He found that the degree of consensus on norms and behavioural expectations partially neutralizes the effects of LMX on empowerment[4].

The importance of human resource management in the future is examined by Berger[5]. Their survey findings suggest that partnerships between employees, guests, and universities along six domains: technology; power paradigms; training and development; compensation; employee relations; and family, society, and work balance, are necessary for hospitality organizations to remain viable in the future.

Before a hospitality organization can begin to concern itself with the future, it must address its present personnel needs. Farrar *et al.*[6] examine the relationship between gender and work-related attribute preferences. Their findings reveal a difference between males (risk avoiders) and females (high achievers), which may prove useful to recruiters attempting to match an individual's needs with job and organizational benefits.

Not only must organizations address the differences between males and females, they must be prepared to meet the challenges associated with increasing diversity in the workplace. In the past, organizations typically responded to diversity by minimizing or eliminating differences. In the future, organizations that fail to acknowledge the full range of variety inherent in their employees and customers will have difficulty surviving[7].

Many hospitality organizations are currently not designed to be successful in meeting the challenges they will face in the not-too-distant future. A diverse workforce is only one of the many changes that can be expected in the next century. Changing customer needs, increased competition, technological advances, and globalization are all current patterns which will lead towards a system-level redesign of tomorrow's hospitality organization[10]. Enz discusses the importance of rethinking how hospitality firms do business and the necessity of organizing in a dynamic environment.

Perhaps one of human resource management's most important functions is establishing an environment that supports the employee. Dienhart and Gregoire[11] suggest that increased job satisfaction, job involvement, and job security may improve an employee's customer focus. It is management's responsibility to have a better understanding of employees and of factors which affect their focus on the services they provide.

Theme 2: service quality and customers

A summary of the articles on the themes of service quality and customers is provided in Table II.

Shane C. Blum
*Organizational trend analysis
of the hospitality industry:
preparing for change*

Table I
People and organizations

Authors	Focus	Sub-theme
Goll[1]	Management creates the environment within an organization. Management must develop operating norms that enhance and protect the values of the organization	Management by values
Borchgrevink and Boster[2]	Leader-member exchange (LMX) is a scale which serves as a measure of the social exchange relationship between two organizational members	Leader-member exchange (LMX)
Sparrowe[3]	The degree of consensus by which group members share norms and behavioural expectations partially neutralizes the effects of LMX on empowerment	Leader-member exchange and employee empowerment
Sparrowe[4]	Psychological empowerment seems to increase satisfaction with promotion opportunities and decrease turnover intentions	Employee empowerment
Berger et al.[5]	Hospitality organizations need to create partnerships with employees, guests and universities	Human resources management
Farrar et al.[6]	Does gender influence the preferred work environment of potential employees?	Personnel selection
Christensen[7]	Organizations that fail to acknowledge the full range of variety inherent in their employees and customers will have difficulty surviving in the future	Diversity in the workplace
Nebel and Ghei[8]	The two major elements that influence a general manager's job are job demands and relationship issues	Job skills
Wood[9]	Identifies ways in which status is used in explaining work place behaviour	Employee status and roles
Enz[10]	Changing customer needs, increased competition, globalization and a diverse workforce are all factors which will lead to a redesign of tomorrow's organizations	Organizational structure
Dienhart and Gregoire[11]	Results indicated that increasing job satisfaction, job involvement and job security may improve an employee's customer focus	Job satisfaction

Through effective human resource management an organization can create an environment which encourages and rewards employees for providing quality service to guests. In order for this to occur, management must know what quality service entails and

Table II
Service quality and customers

Authors	Focus	Sub-theme
Getty and Thompson[12]	Provides a reliable and valid instrument that will measure customer's perceptions of delivered quality within the lodging sector	Service quality
Samenfink[14]	Self-monitoring scales were used to identify and compare service attentiveness and suggestive selling skills in hospitality employees	Service encounter
Francese[18]	Firms which break the traditional rules of bureaucratic structure and managerial behaviour increase responsiveness and customer satisfaction	Customer satisfaction
Lewis et al.[19]	Consumer's choice of hospitality products frequently involves trade-offs among product alternatives. Conjoint analysis can be used to measure consumer preferences	Customer preferences
Francese[22]	Marketing strategies that appealed to the baby-boom generation will have to be revamped to gain the loyalty of the sceptical and cautious post-baby-boom generation	Customer demographics

how it can be properly measured. Getty and Thompson[12] conducted research geared towards creating a reliable and valid instrument to measure customers' perceptions of delivered quality. In addition, Bojanic and Rosen[13] used an instrument for measuring service quality SERVQUAL to examine the association between service quality as perceived by customers and its service determinants.

Management attempts to measure service quality not only from the guest's perspective, but from the employee's as well. It is important for management to be able to quantify the interpersonal skills required by employees in service positions[14]. In two separate studies, Samenfink utilized a self-monitoring scale to determine the theoretical characteristics required of employees to be successful in the service encounter[15]. Once the service encounter is complete, attempts can be made to measure the customer's overall satisfaction. Barsky[16] created his own definition of customer satisfaction along with a practical approach to facilitate its measurement. Almanza *et al.*[17], on the other hand, used Albrecht and Bradford's service attribute matrix to determine attributes leading to customer satisfaction.

All of these models, scales, and surveys used to measure service may seem redundant, but in order to provide quality service it is imperative to know what quality service is. How management defines quality service is insignificant; how the customer defines it is paramount.

Once management is able to identify and provide quality service, the next step is to attempt to attract customers to serve. Measuring how a customer makes a choice between hospitality products is a bit more difficult than some of the other measurement methods previously discussed. The customer's choice of a hospitality product frequently involves trade-offs among multiattribute product alternatives, and a majority of the attributes, such as location, brand name, image, ambience, and amenities, are difficult if not impossible to measure quantifiably. Lewis *et al.*[19] along with others, have used conjoint, or trade-off, analysis to measure customer's choice preferences. Determining customer preferences is important to an organization's success. However, those of us in the hospitality industry must attract customers in the first place. Knowing who the customer is and how to reach him/her is therefore essential. The methods management use to reach its customers depend on the type of customer sought. Vogt *et al.*[20]examine how meeting planners use personal sources of information, such as

prior experience or the advice of others, when making their client's travel arrangements.

Conversely, Mihalik *et al.*[21] compared published sources of information used by Japanese and German international travellers when determining overseas vacation destinations.

In order to reach and attract customers successfully, management must also be aware of the prevailing dynamic socio-demographic characteristics. Francese[22] warns that managers need to realize that the post-baby-boom hospitality consumers will be few in numbers, tough in spirit, pragmatic, and technologically aware. On the other hand, Lago and Poffley[23] address the demographic variability among the elderly with respect to health status, income, and family structure. In either case, awareness of the differences between demographic groups can assist management in identifying the needs of individuals in those groups in order to provide them with quality service.

Theme 3: education and training

Many of the hospitality managers who will be responsible for meeting the challenges of tomorrow are the hospitality management students of today. How well they are prepared to meet these challenges depends on the quality of the current hospitality management curriculum and educators. (A summary of the research themes is given in Table III.)

Although Powers and Riegel[24] foresee a bright future for hospitality education, others, notably Lewis[25] and Pavesic[26], predict its demise. Lewis[25] expresses his concern that hospitality management education has not changed "with the times" over the last ten years and unless programmes begin to pay greater attention to quality teaching and quality, real-world research, he predicts that many programmes will cease to exist. Pavesic[26] expresses similar concerns, and believes that our paradigm concerning the content and delivery of hospitality education needs to change for programmes to survive.

Many of the articles in the HRJ are geared towards members of academia, so it was not surprising to find a host of studies regarding hospitality educators. Shaw and Nightingale[27] discuss the findings of a Carnegie Foundation report on American higher education, which stresses the importance of developing a cultural climate that supports a broader view of scholarship for hospitality education. Kwansa and Farrar[28], and Damitio *et al.*[29] examine ethical behaviour of hospitality educators, while Barrows'[31] work on job satisfaction concludes that

Shane C. Blum
*Organizational trend analysis
of the hospitality industry:
preparing for change*

Table III
Education and training

Authors	Focus	Sub-theme
Lewis[25]	To survive, hospitality programmes must pay greater attention to quality teaching and quality, real-world research that addresses the way companies are really run	Curriculum development
Shaw and Nightingale[27]	Implications of a Carnegie Foundation report are that hospitality educators can, do, and should focus on integration, application and teaching for their scholarly endeavours	Educators
McCleary[30]	Examines potential ethical violations in academic publications and proposes a set of ethical guidelines for writers and researchers in hospitality	Publishing
Mann[36]	To achieve the forecast changes in the classroom caused by increased information technology, the view of education must shift from training to performance and from documentation to the application of knowledge	Advancements in the classroom
Enhagen[38]	Students perceived solid waste disposal, conditions of employment, discrimination issues, employee theft, false advertising, vendor honesty, sanitation and AIDS to be today's most compelling issues in the industry	Student's perceptions
Sciarini and Gardner[40]	Hospitality recruiters were most concerned with a candidate's willingness to relocate, work experiences, and extracurricular involvement when making prescreening decisions	Recent graduates and recruitment
Gamio and Sneed[42]	Determined cross-cultural training practices and needs in US hotel companies to serve as a basis for making recommendations for educational programmes in hospitality management	Training

educators are most satisfied with work achievement factors and least satisfied with support/assistance and compensation factors.

The controversial subject of tenure is examined by Schmidgall and Woods[32] who determined the three most important attributes for gaining tenure were a PhD; a track record of publications; and a track record of good teaching. How often educators get published[33] and in what journals[34] are also important considerations when discussing tenure and promotion.

Producing a continual flow of publications is important, but educators must also keep abreast of the current changes occurring in the classroom as well. Borsenik[33] and Mann[36] address the issue of advancements in information technology and predict what the hospitality education classroom of the twenty-first century will look like. Harris[37] shows how interactive videos are currently being used in the classroom to enhance the student's learning experience.

Just as hotel managers are concerned with their customers' satisfaction, so to must hospitality educators be concerned with their students' satisfaction. After all, the students are the educator's customers. Elfrink *et al.*[37] examined the current usage of outcome measures in hospitality education programmes. Widespread usage was found and most

respondents to the survey believed that assessment would continue to increase, owing to pressure from accrediting bodies and university administrators.

Another measure of students' satisfaction may be how well a hospitality education programme prepares them for their entrance into the workplace. Sciarini and Gardner[40] discovered that hospitality recruiters were most concerned with a candidate's willingness to move, work experience, and extracurricular involvement. Brymer and Pavesic[41] conducted research with recent graduates and determined that academic preparation and quality-of-life issues are very important for industry retention and attrition.

A final educational topic of discussion is the type of training the graduates will receive once they have begun their careers. Gamio and Sneed[42] explore the cross-cultural training practices of US hotel companies, and note that while one-third of their employees were foreign-born, most hotel companies did not provide cross-cultural training. Paulson *et al.*[43] studied the effectiveness of on-the-job training, programmed self-instruction, and simulation training. The study indicates that no one method was superior, and a combination of all three would best maximize the effectiveness of the training.

Shane C. Blum
*Organizational trend analysis
of the hospitality industry:
preparing for change*

Theme 4: finance, strategies and performance

Another major issue addressed by the HRJ is the current financial practices and strategies utilized by mangers in the hospitality industry (see Table IV). Sheel[44] analyses the relationship between a firm's capital structure, its cost of capital, and its stock value as well as the impact of earnings information on common stock returns[45]. Gu[46] focuses his attention on the hospitality investor by reviewing the risk and return on investment in three sectors of the hospitality industry. Findings show that the casino sector was the best performer, followed by the restaurant sector, and then the hotel sector.

The overall financial performance of a property is of importance to investors, managers, employees, and sometimes even guests. Van Dyke and Olsen[47] compared the performance variables of highly profitable hotel operations with those of marginally profitable or losing operations. Five key variables (occupancy rate, rooms sales as percentage of total sales, rooms department labour cost percentage, food cost percentage, and property tax percentage) were found to have a significant relationship with total or consolidated profitability. These variables can be computed relatively easily and can assist the manager in ascertaining the relative financial health of the property.

Most managers of financially successful properties develop and follow a long-term strategic plan. Once the strategy is in place, managers must continually scan sectors of the environment, which are appropriate to the intended strategy, in order to identify trends and changes within each sector[48]. West found that firms espousing low cost or differentiation strategies performed significantly better than firms that focused on one segment of the industry. These higher performing firms also engaged in significantly higher levels of environmental scanning.

Managers must have a clear understanding of the strategic direction of the firm in order to be able to react positively to environmental changes. If, for example, a competitor lowers its prices, management must be able to determine if a matching price reduction is in line with the firm's overall strategy. Haywood[49] describes the key elements of a comprehensive cost management strategy which would assist management with this decision. In addition, Shaw[50] defines the key factors for a pricing decision as demand, competition, and cost: demand sets the ceiling, cost sets the floor, and competition determines where on this continuum the actual price will fall. If, in our example, the competitor does not lower its price below our costs, we may for a time want to follow suit and lower our prices too.

The above pricing example is indicative of a short-run management decision. Whether or not a property should become part of a franchise is an example of a long-term, strategic decision. Poorani and Smith[51] examine whether bed and breakfast owners perceive

Table IV
Finance, strategies and performance

Authors	Focus	Sub-theme
Gu[46]	Reviewed the risk and return of investment in three sectors of the hospitality industry. Findings showed that the casino sector was the best performer, followed by restaurant, and then hotel sector	Capital structure and investment
Van Dyke and Olsen[47]	Compared the performance variables of highly profitable hotel profitable hotel operations and marginally profitable or losing operations to determine which variables have a significant impact on profitability	Financial performance
West[48]	Results indicate that firms espousing low cost or differentiation perform significantly higher than focus firms. Higher performing firms engage in significantly higher levels of environmental scanning	Strategic management
Shaw[50]	Pricing is recognized as both a strategic and tactical tool, and as essential to effective strategic marketing and management in the hospitality industry	Pricing strategies
Poorani and Smith[51]	Concluded that although innkeepers have unmet marketing and sales needs, franchisers have not yet persuaded innkeepers that they can fulfil these needs effectively	Franchising
Chervenak[53]	High-speed, high-capacity fibre optic cable will link the world, and technology will be entrenched in every phase of hotel management, marketing and operations	Communications and technology

the need to join a franchise. Although the owners have unmet marketing and sales needs, franchisers have not yet persuaded the owners that they can fulfil these needs effectively. Powers[52] suggests that reservation systems technology, which can create worldwide reservation networks for independent and small chains, will adversely effect the growth of franchising in the lodging sector.

Other forms of technology are continually changing the way the hospitality industry operates. Chervenak[53] believes that high-speed, high-capacity fibre optics will link the world and change the way hotels communicate with their guests. Interactive, three-dimensional televisions will change how and what guests view in their rooms, while private videoconferencing networks will change the way business is done. One need only examine the impact the Internet has had on the world to agree that technology is one of the most important issues facing the hospitality industry today.

Theme 5: trends analysis, food service sector

Technological changes are not only affecting the hotel sector, but the food service sector as well (Table V). Sanchez *et al.*[54] report that a computerized naive expert system has been developed to assist food service managers with their forecasting. Miller *et al.*[55] believe that technology transfer of management

science techniques is imperative in order to maintain a competitive edge.

Although food service managers need to concern themselves with technological advances there are also a number of other changes occurring in society that may affect the future of the industry. Wallace[56] explores the various demographic, social, and psychological patterns which are likely to be the subject of intense analysis at the turn of the century. Gregorie *et al.*[57] address changes in government, competitive marketing, and the environment and their effects on the school food service sector.

As if all of these potential changes were not enough to deal with, food service managers must also contend with the fact that their workforce is changing as well. Perkins and Cummings[58] determined the part-time employment potential for a community and the inclination to work part-time in the foodservice sector. A reduction in this historically large sector of food service employees will have repercussions throughout the industry and force mangers to explore new alternatives to meet their employment needs.

Perhaps one of the most dramatic changes in the food service sector over the past few decades has been the tremendous increase in the popularity of the fast food sector. Parsa and Khan[60] agree that the quick-service restaurant industry is now truly global. They believe that successful firms can gain

Table V
Trends, analysis, foodservice industry

Authors	Focus	Sub-theme
Miller *et al.*[55]	Applied simple mathematical models to food and beverage operation. Improved forecasting is critical to efficient operations since all production-related costs are impacted by this basic decision	Forecasting
Wallace[56]	Explores the various demographic, social and psychological patterns which will be the subject of intense analysis as we near the year 2000	Trends in food service
Perkins and Cummings[58]	Determined the part-time employment potential for a community and the inclination to work part-time in the food service industry	Food service personnel
Bruce and Nies[59]	Students' knowledge level of nutrition, their attitudes towards nutrition and towards the role of nutrition in commercial food service were measured	Nutrition
Parsa and Khan[60]	Successful quick-service restaurants may gain competitive advantage through segment diffusion, employee empowerment and maximization of brand equity	Quick-service sector
Shanklin *et al.*[63]	A study of selected hotel chains found that a majority of properties had implemented a programme to decrease their volume of waste. The two most important factors for the programme were waste disposal fees and positive public image	Waste management
Hiemstra and Kosiba[64]	Findings indicate that the decline in demand in the food service industry can be largely explained by changes in prices, income and the drop in deductibility of restaurant meals as a business expense	Tax

Shane C. Blum
*Organizational trend analysis
of the hospitality industry:
preparing for change*

a competitive advantage through segment diffusion, employee empowerment, and maximization of brand equity. Firms are also attempting to gain an advantage by moving away from the traditional free-standing restaurant and placing units in airports, shopping malls, and other challenging locations[61].

An increase in the number of restaurants increases customer capacity, but it can also result in an increase in the amount of waste that needs to be handled. Nicholls and Nystuen[62] believe that food service operators and consumers must jointly address the societal demand for conservation, preservation, and ecological issues associated with waste management. Shanklin *et al.*[63] found that the waste management practices implemented most frequently were collapsing cardboard boxes, sorting waste by material, crushing glass, and bailing paper and cardboard.

Theme 6: legal considerations

Shanklin *et al.*[63] also discovered that the two most important factors for implementing a waste management programme were waste disposal fees and positive public image. However, management should also be concerned with the possible legal ramifications of improper disposal of waste materials. Waste disposal is only one of a plethora of legal issues that managers must contend with. A summary of the research on the theme of legal issues is shown in Table VI.

The rights, obligations, and liabilities of the innkeeper and the guest concerning

guest-room use and occupancy are discussed by Alberto[65]. Stauber and Ohlin[66] review the legal environment of exculpatory clauses as they relate to recreational activities provided by hotels, and conclude that in many instances exculpatory clauses remain a legitimate method to reduce the risk of liability. Ohlin and Vickory[67] examine the development of the common law of negligence regarding ski resort liability, while Quinton[68] addresses the liability issues associated with parking an automobile on hotel property.

Examples of liability issues associated with services provided by the hospitality industry are endless. Managers need to keep abreast of any changes in legislation which have the potential to impact their business. The Americans with Disabilities Act (ADA) is a prime example of legislation which has influenced the hospitality industry.

Palmer[69] addresses a number of issues associated with the ADA regarding employees and customers. Under the ADA, management must consider whether a particular applicant or employee is "disabled", whether the person is "qualified" for the job, what the "essential" functions of the job are, and what constitutes "reasonable accommodation" of the disabled individual. Considerations regarding customers include modifications to remove architectural barriers for disabled guests, auxiliary aids necessary to improve the provision of services to disabled guests, and stricter standards applicable to alterations and new construction.

Management must also deal with a myriad of legal concerns associated with able-bodied

Table VI
Legal considerations

Authors	Focus	Sub-theme
Alberto[65]	A discussion of the rights, obligations and liabilities of the innkeeper and the guest is discussed	Liability
Palmer[69]	Implications of the ADA for the hospitality industry are outlined	Americans with Disabilities Act
Enghagen et al.[70]	Provides an overview of the competing interests of employers and employees in relation to electronic monitoring along with a summary of relevant laws and legislation	Employees and the workplace
Wilson et al.[74]	Overbooking which results in walking guests can be considered a breach of contract and may constitute fraud or misrepresentation. Yield management practices need to be scrutinized to bring them into compliance with consumer protection statutes	Yield management
Boyd et al.[72]	Outlines the history and current trends in dram shop legislation throughout the USA	Dram shop laws
Fenich[75]	Federal and local mandates may force Americans' reliance on the automobile for most of their transportation needs to end	Transportation

Shane C. Blum
*Organizational trend analysis
of the hospitality industry:
preparing for change*

employees. Enghagen *et al.*[70] discuss employee privacy rights and electronic monitoring in the workplace. Even proactive, legally aware managers can be victimized by the extraordinarily high rate of costly worker's compensation claims which are prevalent in the hospitality industry[71].

A legal consideration which has plagued the hospitality industry for years is the issue of liquor liability. Boyd *et al.*[70] outline the history of, and current trends in, dram shop legislation throughout the USA. The term "dram shop" law can have extremely divergent meanings from state to state and Enghagen[73] found that some states are expanding their theories of liability, while others are looking at ways to place limits on liability.

While dram shop legislation has received a great deal of attention, legislation regarding the legality of hotel overbooking has remained relatively neglected. Wilson *et al.*[74] warn that when overbooking results in walking guests, a breach of contract has occurred. Under certain circumstances, this may constitute fraud or misrepresentation. Hotel managers need to scrutinize their overbooking practices to ensure that they are in compliance with consumer protection statutes that prohibit unfair and deceptive acts.

Summary

Although six themes have been identified in this review, one theme is stressed throughout; change. Change, whether it be demographic, technological or societal, and how it affects the hospitality industry (Figure 1) is the

Figure 1
Preparing for change

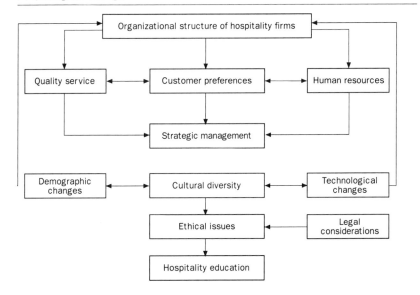

primary subject addressed by the majority of articles in the Hospitality Research Journal from 1989 through 1995. How change proliferates each theme is summarized below:
- In order for hospitality organizations to remain competitive in the future they must become more responsive to the changing needs of their employees and guests. Increased competition, globalization, and a diverse workforce may also cause management to re-evaluate the way their organization is structured.
- Management must be prepared to identify and meet changing customer preferences resulting from changes in the demographic characteristics of our society. These changes may alter the definition of quality service and how it can be provided and measured.
- Changes are affecting hospitality education as well. Some suggest the demise of hospitality programmes if these changes are not successfully met. Ethical, cultural and technological issues are changing the way we educate and train the hospitality managers of the future.
- Hospitality managers must have a clear understanding of the strategic direction of the organization in order to meet the challenges presented by societal changes. Investment, pricing, and other operating decisions will be influenced by the firm's long-term strategic goals.
- Demographic changes are affecting the way managers in the food service sector attempt to attract employees and customers. The continued growth of the quick-service sector and the importance of proper waste management are two other issues which must be addressed in the future.
- Legislative changes such as the Americans with Disabilities Act (ADA) are continually affecting the hospitality industry. Liability issues regarding guest's privacy, employee safety, and liquor sales are some of the key legal concerns facing management.

A summary of the organizational trend analysis of these six themes is presented in Table VII (which appears after the Reference section).

References
(All references are from the *Hospitality Research Journal*)
1 Goll, G., "Management by values: consistency as a predictor of success", Vol. 14 No. 1, 1989, pp. 55-68.
2 Borchgrevink, C.P. and Boster, F.J., "Leader-member exchange: a test of the measurement model", Vol. 17 No.3, 1994, pp. 75-100.

Shane C. Blum
*Organizational trend analysis
of the hospitality industry:
preparing for change*

3 Sparrowe, R.T., "The effects if organizational culture and leader-member exchange on employee empowerment in the hospitality industry", Vol. 18 No.3 and Vol. 19 No.1, 1995, pp. 95-106.

4 Sparrowe, R.T., "Empowerment in the hospitality industry: an exploration of antecedents and outcomes", Vol.17 No.3, 1994, pp. 51-64.

5 Berger, F., Fulford, M.D. and Krazmien, M., "Human resources management in the 21st century: predicting partnerships for profit", Vol. 17 No. 1, 1993, pp. 87-102.

6 Farrar, A.L., Murrmann, S.K. and Vest, J.M., "Profiling managerial entrants to the hospitality industry", Vol. 18 No.1, 1994, pp. 65-76.

7 Christensen, J., "The diversity dynamic: implications for organizations in 2005", Vol. 17 No. 1, 1993, pp. 69-86.

8 Nebel, E.C. and Ghei, A., "A conceptual framework of the hotel's general manager's job", Vol. 16 No.3, 1993, pp. 27-38.

9 Wood, R.C., "Status and hotel and catering work: theoretical dimensions and practical implications", Vol. 16 No.3, 1993, pp. 3-16.

10 Enz, C.A., "Organizational architectures for the 21st century: the redesign of hospitality firms", Vol. 17 No. 1, 1993, pp. 103-12.

11 Dienhart, J.R. and Gregoire, M.B., "Job satisfaction, job involvement, job security, and customer focus of quick-service restaurant employers", Vol. 16 No. 2, 1993, pp. 29-44.

12 Getty, J.M. and Thompson, K.N., "A procedure for scaling perceptions of lodging quality", Vol. 18 No. 2, 1994, pp. 75-96.

13 Bojanic, D.C. and Rosen, L.D., "Measuring service quality in restaurants: an application of the SERVQUAL instrument", Vol. 18 No. 1, 1994, pp. 3-14.

14 Samenfink, W.H., "A quantitative analysis of certain interpersonal skills required in the service encounter", Vol.17 No.2, 1994, pp. 3-16.

15 Samenfink, W.H., "Identifying the service potential of an employee through the use of the self-monitoring scale", Vol. 15 No.2, 1992, pp. 1-10.

16 Barsky, J.D., "Customer satisfaction in the hotel industry: meaning and measurement", Vol. 16 No. 1, 1992, pp. 51-74.

17 Almanza, B.A., Jaffe, W. and Lin, L., "Use of the service attribute matrix to measure consumer satisfaction", Vol. 17 No. 2, 1994, pp. 63-76.

18 Francese, P., "Breaking the rules: delivering responsive service", Vol. 16 No. 2, 1993, pp. 55-74.

19 Lewis, R.C., Ding, S. and Geschke, U., "Using trade-off analysis to measure consumer choices: the full profile method", Vol.15 No. 1, 1991, pp. 75-92.

20 Vogt, C.A., Roehl, W.S. and Fesenmaier, D.R., "Understanding planners' use of meeting facility information", Vol. 17 No. 3, 1994, pp. 119-30.

21 Mihalik, B, Uysal, M. and Pan, M.C., "A comparison of information sources used by vacationing Germans and Japanese", Vol. 18 No. 3 and Vol. 19 No. 1, 1995, pp. 39-46.

22 Francese, P.A., "Rising stars in the consumer constellation: a peer personality profile of the post-baby-boom generation", Vol. 17 No. 1, 1993, pp. 17-28.

23 Lago, D. and Poffley, J.K., "The aging population and the hospitality industry in 2010: important trends and probable services", Vol. 17 No. 1, 1993, pp. 29-26.

24 Powers, T.F. and Riegel, C.D., "A bright future for hospitality education: providing value in the 21st Century", Vol. 13 No. 1, 1989, pp. 295-314.

25 Lewis, R.C., "Hospitality management education: here today, gone tomorrow?", Vol. 17 No.1, 1993, pp. 273-85.

26 Pavesic, D.V., "Hospitality education 2005: curricular and programmatic trends", Vol. 13 No. 1, 1989, pp. 285-88.

27 Shaw, M. and Nightingale, M., "Scholarship reconsidered: implications for hospitality education", Vol. 13 No. 3, 1990, pp. 81-94.

28 Kwansa, F.A. and Farrar, A.L., "A conceptual framework for developing a hospitality educators' code of ethics", Vol. 15 No. 3, 1992, pp. 27-40.

29 Damitio, J.W., Schmidgall, R.S. and Whitney, D.L., "Ethical orientation of hospitality educators", Vol. 16 No. 1, 1992, pp. 75-92.

30 McCleary, K.W., "Ethics in academic publication", Vol. 18 No. 1, 1994, pp. 139-48.

31 Barrows, C.W., "Job satisfaction of hospitality educators", Vol. 16 No. 3, 1993, pp. 39-48.

32 Schmidgall, R.S. and Woods, R.H., "CHRIE member perceptions of tenure requirements in hospitality education programs", Vol. 18 No. 1, 1994, pp. 10 -29.

33 Rutherford, D.G. and Samenfink, W., "Most frequent academic contributors to the hospitality literature", Vol. 16 No. 1, 1992, pp. 23-40.

34 Schmidgall, R.S. and Woods, R.H., "Rating of publishing channels by hospitality faculty", Vol. 16 No. 3, 1993, pp. 89-102.

35 Borsenik, F.D., "Hospitality technology in the 21st Century", Vol. 17 No.1, 1993, pp. 259-72.

36 Mann, S.H., "The hospitality classroom, circa 2005", Vol. 17 No. 1, 1993, pp. 245-58.

37 Harris, K.J., "Interactive video: the instructional tool of the '90s", Vol. 16 No. 2, 1993, pp. 75-94.

38 Enghagen, L.K., "Students' perceptions of ethical issues in the hospitality and tourism industry", Vol. 15 No. 2, 1992, pp. 41-50.

39 Elfrink, J.A, Agbeh A. and Krause, F., "A survey of student assessment in hospitality education: implications for the future", Vol. 17 No. 1, 1993, pp. 259-272.

40 Sciarini, M.P. and Gardner P., "Prescreening of hospitality school graduates: a study of hospitality recruiter decision strategies", Vol. 18 No. 2, 1994, pp. 97-114.

41 Brymer, R.A. and Pavesic, D.V., "Personality characteristics and profiles of hospitality management graduates", Vol. 14 No. 1, 1990, pp. 77-86.

42 Gamio, M.O. and Sneed, J., "Cross-cultural training practices and needs in the hotel industry", Vol. 15 No. 3, 1992, pp. 13-25.

Shane C. Blum
Organizational trend analysis of the hospitality industry: preparing for change

43 Paulson, D.M., Baltzer, L.E. and Cole, R.S., "Methods of educating cashiers in a restaurant teaching laboratory", Vol. 13 No. 2, 1990, pp. 31-44.

44 Sheel, A., "Determinants of capital structure choice and empirics on leverage behavior: a comparative analysis of hotel and manufacturing firms", Vol. 17 No. 3, 1994, pp. 3-16.

45 Sheel, A., "An empirical analysis of anomalies in the relationship between earnings' yield and returns of common stocks: the case of hotel and lodging firms", Vol. 18 No. 3 and Vol. 19 No. 1, 1995, pp. 13-24.

46 Gu, Z., "Hospitality investment return, risk, and performance indexes: a ten-year examination", Vol. 17 No. 3, 1994, pp. 17-26.

47 Van Dyke, T. and Olsen, M.D., "A comparison of performance variables of highly profitable mid-priced hotel/motels with marginally profitable or losing operations", Vol. 13 No. 1, 1989, pp. 13-30.

48 West, J.J., "Strategy, environmental scanning and firm performance: an integration of content and process in the foodservice industry", Vol. 14 No. 1, 1990, pp. 87-100.

49 Haywood, K.M., "A strategic approach to managing costs", Vol. 14 No. 3, 1991, pp. 73-84.

50 Shaw, M., "Positioning and price: merging theory, strategy, and tactics", Vol. 15 No. 2, 1991, pp. 31-40.

51 Poorani, A. and Smith, D.R., "Franchising as a business expansion strategy in the bed and breakfast industry: creating a marketing and development advantage", Vol. 18 No. 2, 1994, pp. 19-28.

52 Powers, T.F., "The advent of the megachain: a case of the emperor's new clothes'", Vol. 15 No. 3, 1992, pp. 1-12.

53 Chervenak, L., "Hotel technology at the start of the new millennium", Vol. 17 No. 1, 1993, pp. 113-20.

54 Sanchez, N., Miller, J., Sanchez, A. and Brooks, B., "Applying expert systems technology to the implementation of a forecasting model in foodservice", Vol. 18 No. 3, 1995, pp. 25-38.

55 Miller, J. and Bloss, B., "Food production forecasting with simple time series models", Vol. 14 No. 3, 1991, pp. 9-22.

56 Wallace, J., "Gateway to the millennium", Vol. 17 No. 1, 1993, pp. 59-68.

57 Gregoire, M., Sneed, J. and Martin, J., "School foodservice: a look to the future", Vol. 17 No.1, 1993, pp. 175-94.

58 Perkins, J. and Cummings, P., "A community economic development survey of part-time labor: implications for the hospitality industry", Vol. 17 No. 3, 1994, pp. 111-18.

59 Bruce, A. and Nies, J., "Nutrition: what hospitality students think and know", Vol. 18 No. 1, 1994, pp. 121-38.

60 Parsa, H. and Khan, M., "Quick-service restaurants of the 21st century: an analytical review of macro factors", Vol. 17 No. 1, 1993, pp. 161-74.

61 Boger, C., "A comparison between different delivery systems of quick service food facilities", Vol. 18 No. 3, 1995, pp. 111-24.

62 Nicholls, L. and Nystuen, C., "Future foodservice waste management", Vol. 17 No. 1, 1993, pp. 231-44.

63 Shanklin, C., Petrillose, M. and Pettay, A., "Solid waste management practices in selected hotel chains and individual properties", Vol. 15 No. 1, 1991, pp. 59-74.

64 Hiemstra, S. and Kosiba, S., 'Recession and tax impacts on the U.S. restaurant industry", Vol.17 No. 2, 1994, pp. 17-23.

65 Alberto, L.M., "Contemporary issues in hotel and restaurant law: use and occupancy of a guest's room-entry by innkeeper", Vol. 14 No.3, 1991, pp. 1-8.

66 Stauber, A. and Ohlin, J.B., 'Exculpatory clauses: legal environment and implications for the hospitality industry", Vol. 17 No. 2, 1994, pp. 77-92.

67 Ohlin, J.B. and Vickory, F.A., "Development of ski resort liability: statutory challenges and implications for the hospitality industry", Vol. 17 No. 2, 1994, pp. 25-38.

68 Quinton, W., "Liability for automobile parking at hotels: the Tennessee case", Vol. 16 No. 1, 1992, pp. 109-20.

69 Palmer, R.A., "The Americans with Disabilities Act: new obligations for hospitality operators", Vol.15 No.2, 1992, pp. 11-20.

70 Enghagen, L.K., Healy, E.P. and Kirschner, R., "The office no longer has walls: privacy rights and electronic monitoring in the workplace", Vol. 18 No. 2, 1994, pp. 115-26.

71 Bandy, M.D., "Workers' compensation claims in the hospitality industry: a comparative study", Vol. 16 No. 3, 1993, pp. 75-88.

72 Boyd, J.N., Vickory, F.A. and Maroney, P.F., "The trends in dram shop laws and how they affect the hospitality industry: balancing competing policy considerations of tort reform and curbing drunk driving", Vol. 15 No. 1, 1991, pp. 25-42.

73 Enghagen, L.K., "New developments in liquor liability law: liability predicated on a general duty of care", Vol. 14 No. 3, 1991, pp. 53-62.

74 Wilson, R.H., Enghagen, L.K. and Sharma, P., "Overbooking: the practice and the law", Vol. 17 No. 2, 1994, pp. 93-108.

75 Fenich, G.G., "Localized ground transportation in the 21st century and its impact on the hospitality industry", Vol. 17 No. 1, 1993, pp. 195-208.

Further reading

Ayala, H., "The unresearched phenomenon of 'hotel circuit'", Vol. 16 No. 3, 1993, pp. 59-68.

Beran, B., "Menu sales mix analysis revisited: an economic approach", Vol. 18 No. 3 and Vol. 19 No. 1, 1995, pp. 125-42.

Shane C. Blum
*Organizational trend analysis
of the hospitality industry:
preparing for change*

Bonn, M.A., Ohlin, J.B. and Brand, R.R., "Quality service issues: a multivariate analysis of association-meeting planner perceptions of Caribbean destinations", Vol. 18 No.1, 1994, pp. 29-48.

Brewer, K.P. and Hurley, R.E., "The staying power of hospitality corporations in the continuing care industry: issues from the front lines", Vol. 17 No. 2, 1994, pp. 107-16.

Brymer, R.A., Rousselle, J.R. and Johns, T.R., "Academic research interests of hospitality corporations", Vol. 14 No. 1, 1990, pp. 1-10.

Callan, R.J., "Development of a framework for the determination of attributes used for hotel selection-indications from focus group and in-depth interview", Vol. 18 No. 2, 1994, pp. 53-64.

Crouch, G.I., "Price elasticities in international tourism", Vol. 17 No. 3, 1994, pp. 27-40.

Damitio, J.W. and Schmidgall, R.S., "Managerial accounting skills for lodging managers", Vol. 14 No. 1, 1990, pp. 69-76.

Damiti, J.W. and Schmidgall, R.S., "Bartering practices in the lodging industry", Vol. 17 No. 3, 1994, pp. 101-10.

Darder, R.J., "An assessment of casino dealer's motivational attitudes", Vol 16 No.2, 1993, pp. 45-54.

Dev, C.S. and Brown, J.R., "Franchising and other operating arrangements in the lodging industry: a strategic comparison", Vol. 14 No. 2, 1991, pp. 22-42.

Diaz, P.E. and Park, J., "The impact of isolation on hospitality employees' job satisfaction and job performance", Vol. 15 No. 3, 1992, pp. 41-50.

Diaz, P.E. and Umbreit, W.T., "Women leaders – a new, beginning", Vol. 18 No. 3 and Vol.19 No. 1, 1995, pp. 47-60.

Dieke, P., "Fundamentals of tourism development: a third world perspective", Vol. 13 No. 2, 1990, pp. 7-22.

Durocher, J.F. and Niman, N.B., "Information technology: management effectiveness and guest services", Vol. 17 No. 1, 1993, pp. 121-32.

Farber, B.M., "Hotel executive teams: balance of power among department heads?", Vol. 18 No. 1, 1994, pp. 15-23.

George, R.T., "Culinary arts students: an empirical study of career and ownership orientation", Vol. 14 No. 1, 1990, pp. 11-22.

Ghiselli, R., Hiemstra, S. and Almanza, B., "Reducing school foodservice waste through the choice of serviceware", Vol. 18 No. 3 and Vol. 19 No. 1, 1995, pp. 3-12

Gilmore, S., "Effectiveness of class discussion in the case method of instruction", Vol. 16 No. 1, 1992, pp. 93-108.

Gilmore, S. and Robson, R.A., "Student perception of laboratory experiences in quantity food production management", Vol. 14 No. 1, 1990, pp. 101-16.

Godbey, G., "Time, work and leisure: trends that will shape the hospitality industry", Vol. 17 No. 1, 1993, pp. 49-58.

Hinkin, T.R. and Tracey, B., "Transformational leadership in the hospitality industry", Vol. 18 No. 1, 1994, pp. 49-64.

Hobson, J.S.P. and Uysal, M., "Infrastructure: the silent crisis facing the future of tourism", Vol. 17 No. 1, 1993, pp. 209-18.

Hsu, C.H.C., "Management development activities and learning interests of university residence hall foodservice managers", Vol. 16 No. 2, 1993, pp. 3-16.

Icenogle, M.L. and Perdue, L.J., "Strategic planning in nonprofit private clubs: fact or fiction", Vol. 18 No. 2, 1994, pp. 137-42.

Ittig, P.T., "Comparisons and projections for business school hospitality programs", Vol. 13 No. 1,1989, pp. 47-54.

Kapoor, S., "Mandatory fast food labeling: support by twelfth graders", Vol. 13 No. 2, 1990, pp. 23-30.

Kohl, J.P. and Stevens, D.B., "Recruitment policies and practices of restaurant, hotels and clubs: a study of the personnel procedures of hospitality firms", Vol 13 No.2, 1990, pp. 45-50.

Kreck, L.A. and Rutherford, D.G., "Measuring of foodservice operational success: entrepreneurs vs. executives", Vol.14 No.3, 1991, pp. 43-52.

Lundberg, C.C., "Forms of resistance by temporary hospitality employees", Vol. 18 No. 2, 1994, pp. 127-36.

Lundberg, C.C., "Productivity enhancement through managing the service encounter", Vol. 14 No. 3, 1991, pp. 63-72.

MacHatton, M.T. and Baltzer, L.E., "Quality personnel selection: using a structured interview guide to improve selection of managers", Vol. 18 No.1, 1994, pp. 77-100.

McCleary, K.W. and Weaver, P.A., "Do business travelers who belong to frequent guest programs differ from those who don't belong?", Vol. 15 No. 3, 1992, pp. 51-64.

Meek, A. and Uysal, M., "Restaurant owners' attitude toward the disabled and the Americans with Disabilities Act", Vol. 15 No. 3, 1992, pp. 65-72.

Miller, J., McCahon, C. and Miller, J., "Foodservice forecasting using simple mathematical models", Vol. 15 No. 1, 1991, pp. 43-58.

Miller, J., McCahon, C. and Miller, J., "Foodservice forecasting: differences in selection of simple mathematical models based on short-term and long-term data sets", Vol. 16 No. 2, 1993, pp. 95-102.

Miller, J.L, "Computer applications in foodservice management education in four-year hospitality management programs", Vol. 13 No. 2, 1990, p. 16.

Mills, S. and Riehle, H., "Foodservice manager 2000", *Hospitality Research Journal* Vol. 17 No. 1, 1993, pp. 147-60.

Moore, R.G. and Wilkinson, S., "Communications technology", Vol. 17 No. 1, 1993, pp. 133-46.

Moore, R.W. and Stefanelli, J., "Power and the hotel controller's role", Vol 13 No.1, 1989, pp. 1-12.

Shane C. Blum
Organizational trend analysis of the hospitality industry: preparing for change

Murphy, M.M., "Vocational career testing contributes to student retention in hospitality programs", Vol. 14 No. 1, 1990, pp. 133-8.

Murrmann, S.K. and Murrmann, K.F., "Employee attitudes toward a nonunion grievance procedure and their influence on unionization", Vol. 16 No. 1, 1993, pp. 41-53.

Parsa, H. and Kahn, M., "Menu trends in the quick service restaurant industry during the various stages of the industry life cycle (1919-1988)", Vol. 15 No. 1, 1991, pp. 93-110.

Partlow, C.G., "Graduate education in hospitality management: implications for curriculum development", Vol. 14 No. 1, 1990, pp. 23-34.

Partlow C.G. and Gregoire, M.B., "Activities of hospitality management program administrators", Vol. 16 No. 3, 1993, pp. 17-23.

Powers, T.F., "The standard world of 2005: a surprise-free scenario", Vol. 16 No. 1, 1992, pp. 1-22.

Pratt, R. and Whitney, D., "Attentional and interpersonal characteristics of restaurant general managers in comparison with other groups of interest", Vol. 15 No. 1, 1991, pp. 9-24.

Reid, R. and Riegel, C., "Supplier relations and selection in the foodservice industry", Vol. 13 No. 2, 1990, pp. 51-62.

Roh, Y.S. and Andrew, W., "U.S. hospitality investment in six potential Eastern European markets", Vol. 17 No. 3, 1994, pp. 41-50.

Ross, G.F., "Management values, work preference ideals, and personality needs as predictors of hospitality industry employee career anchors", Vol. 18 No. 3 and Vol. 19 No.1, 1995, pp. 61-80.

Ross, G.F., "Tourism and hospitality work interest and motivation among potential employees", Vol. 16 No. 2, 1993, pp. 17-28.

Scarpati, S. and Lattuca, F., "Training the handicapped as a resource for the foodservice industry", Vol. 13 No. 1, 1989, pp. 37-46.

Schaffer, J.D. and Litschert, R.J., "Internal consistency between strategy and structure: performance implications in the lodging industry", Vol. 14 No. 1, 1990, pp. 35-54.

Seaton, A., "Cocktail culture in the 1920s and 1930s: prefiguring the postmodern", Vol. 18 No. 2, 1994, pp. 35-52.

Shanklin, C., "Ecology age: implications for the hospitality and tourism industry", Vol. 17 No. 1, 1993, pp. 219-25.

Singh, A. and Gu, Z., "Diversification, financial performance, and stability of foodservice firms", Vol. 18 No. 2, 1994, pp. 3-18.

Sparks, B., "Communicative aspects of the service encounter", Vol. 17 No. 2, 1994, pp. 25-38.

Wicks, B, Uysal, M. and Kim, S., "The effects of lodging prices on visitors' demand: Everglades National Park", Vol. 17 No. 2, 1994, pp. 51-62.

Wilson, R.H., "Combining hotel promotions, discount packages, and yield management systems: make sure it's legal", Vol. 15 No. 2, 1992, pp. 21-30.

Wright, P.C., "Validating hospitality curricula within association-sponsored certification programs: a qualitative methodology and a case study", Vol. 14 No.1, 1990, pp. 117-32.

Shane C. Blum
*Organizational trend analysis
of the hospitality industry:
preparing for change*

Table VII

Organizational trend analysis of the hospitality industry; preparing for change – themes, subthemes and observations based on a review of 135 entries (1989-1995) in the *Hospitality Research Journal*

Themes	Sub-themes	Observations
Theme 1: People and organizations	Management by values; leader-member exchange (LMX); leader-member exchange and employee empowerment; employee empowerment; human resources management; personnel selection; diversity in the workplace; job skills, employee status and roles; organizational structure; job satisfaction	In order for hospitality organizations to remain competitive in the future they must become more response to the changing needs of their employees and guests. Increased competition, globalization, and a diverse workforce may also cause management to re-evaluate the way their organization is structured
Theme 2: Service quality and customers	Service quality, service encounter, customer satisfaction; customer preferences; customer demographics	Management must be prepared to identify and meet changing customer preferences resulting from changes in the demographic characteristics of our society. These changes may alter the definition of quality service and how it can be provided and measured
Theme 3: Education and training	Curriculum development; educators; publishing; advancements in the classroom students' perceptions; recent graduates and recruitment; training	Changes are affecting hospitality education as well. Some suggest the demise of hospitality programmes if these changes are not met successfully. Ethical, cultural and technological issues are changing the way we educate and train the hospitality managers of the future
Theme 4: Finance, strategies and performance	Capital structure and investment; financial performance; strategic management; pricing strategies, franchising, communications and technology	Hospitality managers must have a clear understanding of the strategic direction of the organization in order to meet the challenges presented by societal changes. Investment, pricing, and other operating decisions will be influenced by the firms long-term strategic goals
Theme 5: Trends analysis, foos service industry	Forecasting trends in food service; food service personnel; nutrition;quick-service sector; waste management; tax implications	Demographic changes are affecting the way managers in the food service sector attempt to attract employees and customers. The continued growth of the quick-service sector and the importance of proper waste management are two other issues which must be addressed in the future
Theme 6: Legal considerations	Liability; Americans with Disabilities Act; employees and the workplace; yield management; dram shop laws; transportation	Legislative changes such as the Americans with Disabilities Act (ADA) are continually affecting the hospitality industry. Liability issues regarding guest's privacy, employee safety; and liquor sales are some of the key legal concerns facing management

Diverse developments in travel and tourism marketing: a thematic approach

Clark Hu

Research Manager (North America) Worldwide Hospitality and Tourism Trends, William F. Harrah College of Hotel Administration, University of Nevada, Las Vegas, USA

Reviews developments in travel and tourism marketing as reflected by articles published in the *Journal of Travel and Tourism Marketing* over a four-year period from the journal's inception in 1992-1995. Identifies five main themes (economic psychology, market segmentation and travel patterns, strategic marketing, technological advances and travel and tourism communications) and related subthemes that portray a pattern of diverse research and development relating to the practice of travel and tourism marketing.

Introduction

The purpose of this review is to identify recent developments of travel and tourism marketing that have been published in the *Journal of Travel and Tourism Marketing* from 1992 to 1995. This publishes articles of interest to both academics and practitioners. The articles focus on travel and tourism as related to marketing management practices, applied research studies, critical reviews on major issues, and business and government policies affecting travel and tourism marketing.

The review takes a thematic approach to present trends and highlights key threads, in table format, reflecting developments of travel and tourism marketing in:

1. economic psychology;
2. market segmentation and travel patterns;
3. strategic marketing;
4. technological advances; and
5. travel/tourism communications.

Theme 1: economic psychology of travel and tourism

A large number of articles reviewed involve studies in the economic psychology as described by Raaij and Crotts[1]. As shown in Table I, the first theme focuses on this issue in travel and tourism with emphases in three areas:

1. consumer behaviour;
2. choice modelling and decision-making; and
3. service quality and satisfaction.

Raaij and Crotts argue that economic psychology is emerging as a promising area of travel and tourism research and they overview the theoretical background and developments of economic psychology that are relevant to travel and tourism. Economic psychology is an interdisciplinary study that underlies the consumption of products, services, and other economic behaviours. In Raaij and Crotts's article, they discuss a variety of economic-psychological applications in tourism including product perception, consumer behaviour, consumer decision making,

household production, advertising effects, business behaviour, tax behaviour, and consumer satisfaction. They also develop a theoretical framework for understanding the function and processing of information in vacation decision making. Following the same thread, van Rekom[2] elaborates that the motives of tourists are deeply rooted in their pattern of expectations, goals, and psychologically added values. He uses laddering technique to investigate this pattern and provided a basis for positioning strategies.

Dimanche and Havitz[3] state that consumer behaviour research constitutes a cornerstone of marketing strategy and practice. They examine the current literature related to four prevalent topical areas associated with consumer behaviour in recreational and touristic contexts: ego involvement, loyalty and commitment, family decision making, and novelty seeking. In order to understand consumer behaviour in tourism better, a number of choice models have been developed or used to examine tourist decisions. Examples are the "value stretch model" by Mansfeld[4]; the LOGIT model of qualititive choice by Costa and Manente[5]; the analytic hierarchy process (AHP) method with multiattribute decision model (MDM) by Tsaur and Tzeng[6]; the AHP method with LOCAT model by Moutinho and Curry[7]; a customized Multinomial Logit (MNL) model by Hume et al.[8].

Decision making, another area under this main theme, also draws significant attention from researchers. Seaton and Tagg[9] explore family vacation behaviour in Belgium, France, Italy and the UK and examines the perceived roles of children in vacation decision making and the relationship between these roles and vacation satisfactions. Gitelson and Kerstetter[10] study the extent to which friends and/or relatives influence the travel decision-making process beyond the role of information provider. Their results indicated that friends and/or relatives shape behaviour in a more direct fashion than previously documented. Stewart and Stynes[11] note that many common assumptions employed in decision modelling are violated in more complex, long-range choices, which are common in tourism. They propose a dynamic model of complex choice to study tourism decision making behaviour. Madrigal[12] examines family members' perceptions in vacation decision making. The results generally support the view that most vacation decision making between spouses is syncratic and that children's perceived influence was found to be positively related to their age and parents' years of education.

Service quality and satisfaction issues also receive some attention. Ostrowski *et al.*[13] examines issues related to service quality in the commercial airline industry. They found that current levels of service quality are low resulting in low levels of customer loyalty and that significant differences exist between business and leisure travellers' perceptions of

Table I
Economic psychology of travel and tourism

Authors	Focus	Sub-theme
Raaij and Crotts[1]	Theoretical background and applications of economic psychology in travel and tourism; framework information processing in vacation decision making	Economic behaviour; economic psychology in general
van Rekom[2]	Investigates tourists pattern of expectations, goals and psychological added values	Laddering technique
Dimanche and Havitz[3]	Examines four prevalent areas associated with consumer behaviour in recreational and touristic contexts	Ego involvement, loyalty and commitment, family decision making, and novelty seeking
Mansfeld[4]	Uses "value stretch" model to expose the destination-choice behaviour of tourists	North-West London Jewish community
Costa and Manente[5]	Uses LOGIT model to investigate the main characteristics of the visitors and delineate marketing policies	Marketing historic centres
Tsaur and Tzeng[6]	Perception of hotel attributes that affect the selection of tourist hotels	Analytic hierarchy process (AHP) method; multiattribute decision making (MDM analysis; service quality
Moutinho and Curry[7]	Site location analysis and selection in tourism using spreadsheet (LOCAT) models and the analytic hierarchy process (AHP)	Rule based expert systems
Hume *et al.*[8]	Models transport choice behaviour as a function of respondents' perceptions of travel mode attributes using a multinomial logit model	Travel mode between Perth and Sydney or Melbourne, Australia
Seaton and Tagg[9]	Examines the perceived roles of children in vacation decision making and the relationship between these roles and vacation satisfactions	Reviews the literature on family roles in consumer decision-making and vacation choice/experience
Gitelson and Kerstetter[10]	Determines the extent to which friends and/or relatives influence the travel decision-making process beyond the role of information provider	Non-locals visiting three historic site in Pennsylvania, USA
Stewart and Stynes[11]	Uses verbal protocol methods to propose a dynamic model of complex choice of the seasonal home location decision	Reviews decision making research
Madrigal[12]	Examines spouses' perceptions of the relative influence exerted by family members across eight vacation subdecisions	Predicting parents' perceptions of children's influence in vacation decision making
Ostrowski *et al.*[13]	Examines issues related to service quality in the commercial airline industry	Business and leisure travellers' perceptions of service quality
Luk et al.[14]	Investigates tourists' expectations on the quality of organized tour service and the influences of cultural values on quality expectations	Use of cultural values in segmenting the international tourism market
Laws and Ryan[15]	Uses the diary method to generate insights into the nature of the service delivery	Satisfaction/dissatisfaction with the flight service

Clark Hu
*Diverse developments in
travel and tourism marketing:
a thematic approach*

service quality and between travellers on different airlines. Luk *et al.*[14] examine tourists' expectations on the quality of organized tour service and the influences of cultural values on quality expectations. Their cross-cultural investigation explores the use of cultural values in segmenting the international tourism market. The results indicates that sociability is more likely to affect tourists" expectations than other value factors. Laws and Ryan[15] illustrate the use of the diary method by the participant observers and argue that this method generates insights into the nature of the service delivery and supports the concept of satisfaction as a "consumerist gap" between anticipation and service delivery.

Theme 2: market segmentation and travel patterns

One of the most important and challenging issues affecting travel and tourism marketing is to understand where the tourists come from and what are their travel patterns. The second main theme highlights recent developments in these two areas: market segmentation and travel patterns (Table II).

For market segmentation, new methodologies have been developed to increase the segmentation accuracy. Thus, marketers are able to approach travellers with effective marketing strategies. Johar and Sirgy[16] introduce an analytic technique, segment congruence analysis, to help the travel/tourism marketer determine the actionability of viable or potential tourist segments. The analysis shows that benefit segmentation is more predictive of tourists' choice than psychographic segmentation. Mazanec[17] develops a neural network model to classify tourists. He uses a set of input variables (descriptors such as demographic, socioeconomic, or behavioural attributes) to train the model and output segment membership. He argues that neural nets may surpass discriminant analysis in determining the correct segment affiliation. Dimanche *et al.*[18] demonstrate the potential usefulness of the involvement profile scale to segment tourists on the basis of their involvement profiles with touristic activities. Other developments using more traditional segmentation approaches are the application of multivariate techniques conducted by Weaver *et al.*[19] to position hotels within the business travel market.

It is also evident in the studies by Conlin[20] and Davis *et al.*[21] that segmentation strategy has become increasingly important for successful marketing planning in the tourism industry. That is, segmentation helps effective control of how advertising dollars can be allocated to maximize positive impacts to the economic base. This concept applies to regional as well as to national travel markets as seen in the articles of Lang *et al.*[22] and Oppermann[23].

Travel patterns are broad areas for travel research ranging from outbound/inbound travel to the issues of travel expenditures and uses of travel information. Wang and Sheldon[24] discuss China's outbound travel. Cai *et al.*[25] study consumers' expenditure patterns for tourism products. Roehl and Fesenmaier[26] model the influence of information obtained at state welcome centres on visitor expenditures in Indiana. The results from these studies bear marketing and managerial implications for improving travel operations and increasing economic benefits. The family life cycle (FLC) has received research attention in recent years in travel marketing. Oppermann[27] discusses various aspects of travel patterns with respect to the FLC and Bojanic[28] determines the vacation attributes preferred by residents (segmented by FLC) of the USA when they engage in overseas travel.

Some industry-specific travel patterns are found in this review. Rutherford and Kreck[31] explore the extent to which different groups of convention attendees add tourism or recreation activities to the convention experience and the amount of money they spend on such activities. Sheldon[32] examines the phenomenon of incentive travel and gives insight into its use by major US corporations. His results show that corporations with a strong national or international presence, and those having a large in-house corporate travel department, are more likely to use incentive travel.

Other travel patterns involved in international tourism are also found. Crouch[33] investigates the pattern of international travel and tourism demand influenced by promotional activities. The results suggest a stronger link between promotion and demand in international tourism than has been previously studied. Covington *et al.*[34] studied the role of income in determining international tourism demand for the USA as a travel destination. Empirical findings indicate that tourism demand is responsive to the cost of travelling but that income plays a greater role in tourism demand. The results also indicate that, with respect to income, tourism demand is increasing but at a decreasing rate.

Clark Hu
Diverse developments in
travel and tourism marketing:
a thematic approach

Table II
Market segmentation and travel patterns

Authors	Focus	Sub-theme
Johar and Sirgy[16]	Demonstrate that the benefits segments in the choice of Maine as a tourism destination are the most actionable segments, compared to psychographic and life-style segments	Uses segment congruence analysis
Mazanec[17]	Market segments in travel and tourism using neural network model	Cluster and discriminant analyses
Dimanche et al.[18]	Demonstrate the potential usefulness of the involvement profile scale to segment tourists based on their involvement profiles with touristic activities	Cluster analysis
Weaver et al.[19]	Identifies segments within the business travel market based on criteria business travellers use to choose their hotels	Factor analysis
Conlin[20]	Discusses the historical development and effect of national tourism strategy and policies for Bermuda	A single segment tourism destination
Davis et al.[21]	Develops four tourist segments using tourist attracting attributes	Economic growth and promotional strategies
Lang et al.[22]	Segments the Japanese female travel market	Cluster analysis
Oppermann[23]	Uses a regionally differentiated approach in national tourism marketing and forecasting	Balances tourism flows
Wang and Sheldon[24]	Examines the determinants, trends and characteristics of China's outbound travel	Business travel
Cai et al.[25]	Examines leisure travel expenditure patterns of households	Segmentation strategies
Roehl and Fesenmaier[26]	Models the influence of information obtained at state welcome centres on visitor expenditures in Indiana	
Bojanic[27]	Determines the vacation attributes preferred by US residents in overseas travel pattern	Modernized family life cycle (FLC)
Opperman[28]	Proposes a modernized family life cycle (FLC) which reduces the number of non-classifiable cases	Discusses various aspects of travel patterns with respect to FLC
Menguc[29]	An empirical study on major attributes of residents living in Istanbul, Turkey when purchasing a domestic tour	The role a travel agency plays in vacation planning
Ross[30]	Examines motivational responses of 400 backpacker visitors to the Wet Tropics region of Northern Australia	Levels of Maslow's hierarchy of needs
Rutherford and Kreck[31]	Explores the extent to which different groups of convention attendees add tourism or recreation activities to the convention experience	Tourism spending patterns
Sheldon[32]	Examines the phenomenon of incentive travel and gives insight into its use by major US corporations	Characteristics of incentive travel
Crouch[33]	Investigates marketing expenditure elasticities of demand to provide stronger evidence of the link between promotion and demand in international tourism	The pattern of international travel and tourism demand
Covington et al.[34]	Investigates the role of income in determining international tourism demand for the US as a travel destination	Tourism demand estimation

Clark Hu
*Diverse developments in
travel and tourism marketing:
a thematic approach*

Theme 3: strategic marketing

It is apparent that a successful travel and tourism operation must not only understand who the customers are and how they behave but also know what the products/services are and how to market them. The third main theme, as presented in Table III, is strategic marketing that consists of the following key developments:

- travel packaging;
- promotion, advertising, and imaging;
- distribution channel and strategic alliances.

Hooper[35] explains travel packaging as a marketing tool in the form of price bundling. Particular emphasis is placed on the impact of packaging on consumer decision making. The developed framework is used to analyse conflicting claims about the future for the fully-inclusive tour.

In most hospitality operations, intangibility is a barrier to the formation of positive customer perceptions. Several innovative advertising techniques have been suggested by scholars and practitioners to overcome the impact of intangibility on potential guests' learning processes, including tangibilizing the advertising message, enhancing the level of information vividness, and adopting the reliability theme and so on[36]. In the hotel sector, Luk *et al.*[36] attempt to investigate the features of advertising strategies commonly employed by hotel marketers and to provide substantial evidence to test the awareness of the implications of generic service characteristics for effective advertising of hotel service. In the travel industry, Uysal *et al.*[37] suggest that the creative use of marketing research is essential for the tourist business to grow and survive. They develop a Markov model to analyse trip switching and predicting market share for a given trip type. The resulting information can be used to target advertising campaigns. Gartner[38] argues that understanding the different techniques utilized to form destination images is necessary to developing an image consistent with what a destination has to offer. He presents a typology of the different image formation agents, describes the process of touristic image formation and provides recommendations for selecting the appropriate image formation mix.

Other aspects relating to the advertising and promotion are measurement of the advertising effectiveness, the media selection, and

Table III
Strategic marketing

Authors	Focus	Sub-theme
Hooper[35]	Emphasizes the impact of travel packaging on consumer decision making	Price bundling as a marketing strategy
Luk *et al.*[36]	Investigates the features of advertising strategies commonly employed by hotel marketers	Generic service characteristics for effective advertising of hotel service
Uysal *et al.*[37]	Developing a Markov model to analyse trip switching and predicting market share for a given trip type	Advertising campaigns
Gartner[38]	Develops a theoretical basis for the touristic image formation process	Selecting the appropriate image formation mix
Schoenbachler *et al.*[39]	Examines the use of the split-run assessment technique in state tourism advertising research	Advertising effectiveness
Snepenger and Snepenger[40]	Examines media selection practices by tourism businesses competing in Alaska	Market structure analysis
Wicks and Schuett[41]	Examines how regional travellers request and use the travel brochures	Travel propensity and expenditures
Duke and Persia[42]	Discusses differences of customers within the channel of distribution in the escorted tour	Escorted tour as a market segment
Selin[43]	Provides a framework for understanding the trend towards co-operative marketing strategies in tourism	Collaborative alliances as a management strategy
McKercher[44]	Proposes a new qualitative strategic market portfolio analysis model destination-market matrix (DMM) for the tourism industry; NEST analysis	

the use of travel brochures. Schoenbachler *et al.*[39] examine the use of the split-run assessment technique in state tourism advertising research and use this technique to evaluate state advertsing effectiveness. Snepenger and Snepenger[40] examine media selection practices by tourism businesses competing in Alaska. Media use decisions focus on the choice of television, national magazines, radio, newspapers, outdoor advertising, and a regional travel magazine. Media mix decisions explore what combinations of these six media firms are utilized. Wicks and Schuett[41] examine how regional travellers request and use this material, specifically focusing on the relationships between brochure use and propensity to travel and travel expenditures. Their results suggest that, in general, brochure requests are marginally related to high conversions.

Research regarding distribution channels and strategic alliances has increased in recent years. Duke and Persia[42] study attributes important to escorted tour participants to explore the differences between clients of tour operators and clients of travel agents. They found that customers purchasing directly from operators valued experience with the tour company and personal recommendations. Agency clients valued booking through agents along with information from guidebooks and tourist bureau. Differences are discussed in terms of different segments of customers within the channel of distribution. Selin[43] provides a framework for understanding this trend towards collaborative action. Constraints to collaboration are identified as well as societal forces prompting collaborative responses from tourism stakeholders. He clams that rapid economic, social, and political changes are providing powerful incentives for tourism interests to recognize their interdependences and to engage in joint decision-making.

A final aspect of the strategic marketing sub-theme relates to McKercher's research[44].

He proposes a new qualitative strategic market portfolio analysis model for the tourism industry that depicts the complex interrelationship between a destination and the many markets it serves. His destination-market matrix (DMM) is a descriptive 2 × 2 matrix that depicts six key market factors in a conceptually simple, yet highly descriptive manner. He argues that tourism's needs are best suited by adopting a market focus. By analyzing the contents of the matrix, called a NEST analysis, powerful insights can be gained into the current health of a destination area and its future strategic marketing needs.

Theme 4: technological advances

Table IV describes the recent development in technological advances of travel and tourism marketing. Four articles selected from the literature review represent the emerging facets of these technological developments.

Go and Williams[45] highlight the channel system in tourism in the light of the impact of recent developments in technology. The changes in the tourism channel system are discussed in terms of demand and supply and how information technology is affecting the marketing distribution channel for tourism producers. The focus of this analysis relates to the pooling of individual energies through, and the promotion of co-operation in, supplier marketing efforts with compatible partners, so that supplier output is more available and accessible to target markets. Co-operation through networking in the tourism channel system provides the key to gaining a competitve edge in the tourism industry[45]. Kingsley and Fesenmaier[46] study a new channel for disseminating travel information, the multimedia kiosk, and presents an overview of the technology underlying multimedia kiosks used in the tourism industry. Multimedia travel information kiosks have been placed in a number of locations

Table IV
Technological advances

Authors	Focus	Sub-theme
Go and Williams[45]	Highlights the marketing distribution channel system in tourism	Information technology
Kingsley and Fesenmaier[46]	Overviews the technology underlying multimedia kiosks used in the tourism industry	Analyses and categorizes travel information systems
Deng and Ryan[47]	Describes the current and intended future use of computer reservations systems (CRS) by Canadian travel agents	CRS as a marketing tool
Robinson and Keamey[48]	Examines the development and role of database marketing (DBM) in the airlines	DBM in the travel industry in general

Clark Hu
*Diverse developments in
travel and tourism marketing:
a thematic approach*

including in hotel lobbies, at tourist attractions and state welcome centres. Their uses range from educational and training tools to information directories and point-of-sale systems. For the tourism industry, multimedia kiosks are alternatives to traditional travel literature and brochures. They can efficiently and effectively organize and present large amounts of information, promote travel destinations, and perform various tasks (e.g., dispense travel coupons, make reservations, record transactions, etc.). Deng and Ryan[47] describe the current and intended future use of computer reservations systems by Canadian travel agents. They argue that there is an increasing awareness of how these systems might be used for both administrative and management functions within the travel agency, and as a marketing tool for "customizing" travel arrangements to meet individual needs. The type of use being made of these systems seems unrelated to size of the agency, or the numbers of years they have been trading[47].

Finally, much potential is attributed to the use of database marketing. Robinson and Keamey[48] examine the development and role of database marketing in the travel industry in general and in the airlines in particular. The airline industry has effectively merged its information with that from

other travel services to serve consumers better and to increase marketing efficiency. Computer reservation systems (CRS), frequent flyer programmes (FFP), and yield management (YM) are integrated through database marketing to gain competitive advantage in the marketplace[48].

Theme 5: travel/tourism communications

The last main theme is marketing communications in travel and tourism. This topic includes many sub-themes. They are shown in Table V and primarily categorized in three areas:
1 communication channels;
2 communication effectiveness; and
3 information acquisition and search.

According to Reid and Reid[49], three marketing communication elements are critical in building and retaining repeat visitors: external, internal and word-of-mouth messages. Their article provides a conceptual model that links these communications elements to the phenomenon of repeat travel purchase behaviour. They emphasize the importance of repeat customers to tourism services and explore why and how each type of marketing communication has an impact

Table V
Travel/tourism communications

Authors	Focus	Sub-theme
Reid and Reid[49]	Provides a conceptual model that links three marketing communication elements: external, internal and word-of-mouth messages to the phenomenon of repeat travel purchase behaviour	Building and retaining repeat visitors
Hsieh and O'Leary[50]	Uses cluster analysis to identify UK long haul pleasure travellers by four groups of communication channels: word-of-mouth, brochures/pamphlets, travel agents, and combination packages	Market segmentation
Noe et al.[51]	Examines the communication effectiveness of environmental messages in relation to demographic, trip characteristics and possible management actions	Tourism behaviour in a natural recreation area
Fesenmaier and Vogt[52]	Identifies information sources most often used and the level of helpfulness of each information source for planning trips	Evaluates alternative marketing communication strategies simulation analyses
Goossens[53]	Examines the tourist's external information search process in tour brochures for vacation planning	Advertising effect; consumer behaviour
Vogt et al.[54]	Examines pre-trip information acquisition for short Midwest trips	Functional and aesthetic information needs in tourism consumption
Andereck and Caldwell[55]	Determines the relationship between the characteristics of visitors to an attraction and information source importance ratings	Demographic and trip characteristics

Clark Hu
*Diverse developments in
travel and tourism marketing:
a thematic approach*

on these visitors. Hsieh and O'Leary[50] examine communication channels as a segmentation base to understand what kind of information sources travellers use, and whether potential travellers in different groups vary in terms of sociodemographics, travel characteristics, media habits, and psychographic behaviour. Using cluster analysis, four groups of communication channels are identified for UK long haul pleasure travellers: word-of-mouth, brochures/pamphlets, travel agents, and combination packages. Their results show that this segmentation is viable and that implications exist for promotional strategies, distribution channels, and market positioning.

Noe *et al.*[51] investigate the effectiveness of environmental messages in relation to demographic, trip characteristics and possible management actions. Three environmental messages were designed to encourage positive behaviour and reduce environmentally destructive behaviour in a natural recreation area. Their research revealed that communication effectiveness can be enhanced by manipulating various symbols in messages. They found that communication effectiveness is also dependent on demographic and trip characteristics as well as environmental orientations of users.

Research in travel and tourism has identified the information sources used most often by travellers to develop more efficient communications with potential tourists. Fesenmaier and Vogt[52] investigate the extent to which travellers actually use various information sources for planning Midwest vacations. The demographic analyses indicate that segments exist which derive greater utility from particular travel information sources. Goossens[53] examines the tourist's external information search process for vacation planning in a field experiment. The results indicate that tour brochures with experiential texts, and a reader's instruction to activate imagery, did not cause more external search than brochures without such information. Vogt *et al.*[54] examine functional and aesthetic information needs in a tourism consumption context, specifically pre-trip information acquisition for short Midwest trips. Destination selection information needs are shown to be at the core of information acquisition with product knowledge, aesthetic imagery and planning efficiency needs at the "periphery". Information sources about a product or service potentially affect a tourist's purchase decision. Andereck and Caldwell[55] determine the

relationship between the characteristics of visitors to an attraction and information source importance ratings. They conclude that word-of-mouth information is rated most important, followed by past experience and other media sources.

Concluding observations

Jurowski and Olsen[56] use content analysis to identify patterns of activity that exist in the context of the general environment of the tourism industry and possible trends emanating from this environment that are likely to shape the structure of the industry over the next ten years. The major trends identified and explored are: changing consumer preferences; smaller scale tourist attractions appealing to more niche oriented segments, greater local involvement in tourism development decisions; more precise targeting and aggressive marketing; greater use of technology in marketing and servicing tourists; increased alliances especially among small firms; greater and more aggressive involvement of industry associations; and greater international expansion in the developing world. This review reinforces many of the issues identified by Jurowski and Olsen, and summary observations on the five main themes are given below (and in Table VI).

- Evidence suggests that the economic psychology of travel and tourism will remain the mainstay of research and developmental interests. Travel marketers will continue discovering new methods to model tourists' behaviours and choices more accurately. The decision-making process of travel behaviour seems likely to attract more attention in the future. It is also recognized that the perceived quality of travel products and services directly links to the customer satisfaction/dissatisfaction that ultimately dictates the profitability of tourism organizations.

- As new methods for market segmentation are tested and developed, travel and tourism markets will be segmented more efficiently and marketing practices and strategies will be adopted accordingly (i.e., market targeting or customer retention). On the other hand, research in travel patterns will continue to be diverse at regional, national, and international levels, interacting with studies of market segments. Tourist expenditure patterns and the growth of the tourism economy seem to be major concerns that have implications for tourism policies.

- The review indicates that advertising-related issues receive more attention in

Clark Hu
Diverse developments in
travel and tourism marketing:
a thematic approach

Table VI

Diverse developments and emerging trends in travel and tourism maketing research – themes, subthemes and observations based on a review of 80 entries (1992-1995) in the *Journal of Travel and Tourism Marketing*

Themes	Subthemes	Observations
Theme 1: economic psychology	Theoretical background and applications of economic psychology; framework information processing in decision making; consumer destination/transportation choice behaviour (including decision making); perceptions/expectations of travel products/services; service quality and consumer satisfaction site location analysis; choice modelling	Evidence suggests that economic psychology of travel and tourism will remain the mainstream of research and developmental interests. Travel marketers will continue discovering new methods to model tourists' behaviours and choices more accurately. The decision-making process of travel behaviour will especially draw more attention in the future. It is also recognized that the perceived quality of travel products and services directly links to the customer satisfaction/dissatisfaction that ultimately dictates the profitability of tourism organizations
Theme 2: market segmentation and travel patterns	New segmentation methodologies; benefit segmentation; involvement profile scale; attribute-based segmentation; travel market identification; tourism forecasting based on market segments; outbound/inbound travel patterns, tourist expenditure patterns; overseas travel pattern; family life cycle (FLC); study of backpacker visitors (customer loyalty); the phenomenon of incentive travel and characteristics of incentive travel; the relations between marekting expenditures and international tourism	As new methods for market segmentation are used and developed, travel and tourism markets will be segmented more efficiently and marketing practices strategies will be implemented more effectively for many purposes (i.e., market targeting or customer retention). On the other hand, research in travel patterns will continue to be diverse at regional, national, and international levels interacting with studies of market segments. Tourist expenditure patterns and the growth of tourism economy seem to be major concerns that have implications for tourism policies
Theme 3: strategic marketing	The impact of travel packaging on consumer decision making; advertising and promotion strategies; developing a Markov model to analyse trip switching and predicting market share; touristic image formation process; media selection practices; distribution channels; co-operative marketing strategies in tourism; a new qualitative strategic market portfolio analysis model – destination-market matrix (DMM)	The literature review indicates that advertising-related issues receive more attention in research. The travel packaging and pricing bundling require further investigations for strategic marketing uses. DMM is a promising and useful tool to understand the structure of travel industry. Strategic alliances among travel suppliers are encouraged to utilize various distribution channels for marketing and managerial purposes
Theme 4: technological advances	Marketing distribution channel system; information technology; technology underlying multimedia kiosks; the current and future use of computer reservations systems (CRS); database marketing (DBM) in the travel industry	The technological innovations continue to be very important for travel operations to gain competitive advantages over their competitors. Information technology is the key to success for today and to survive for tomorrow. Database marketing becomes a reality of marketing practices. Advanced data-mining techniques (i.e., neural nets) will add more powerful tools in travel and tourism marketing
Theme 5: travel/tourism communications	Marketing communication channels (word-of-mouth, etc.); Building and retaining repeat visitors; measurement of communication effectiveness; the use, search, acquisition,and identification of travel information sources; relationship between the tourist characteristics and information source importance ratings	Because travel products and services have the generic characteristic of intangibility, how to use appropriate communication channels to overcome the barrier becomes a focal point of research. Recent literature shows that the main research interest is in travel information sources to improve tourist communications with travel operators. A few attempts have been made to increase research scope (e.g. measuring communication effectiveness and marketing communication channels). More studies are needed to advance the understanding of communication mechanism for systematic and strategic uses

Clark Hu
*Diverse developments in
travel and tourism marketing:
a thematic approach*

research. The travel packaging and pricing bundling require further investigations for strategic marketing uses. Destination-Market Matrix (DMM) is a promising and useful tool to understand the structure of the travel sector better. Strategic alliances among travel suppliers are encouraged to utilize various distribution channels for marketing and managerial purposes.

• Technological innovations continue to be very important for travel operations in terms of competitive advantages over their competitors. Database marketing has become more widely adopted and advanced data-ming techniques (i.e., neural nets) will add more powerful tools in travel and tourism marketing research.

• Because travel products and services have the generic characteristic of intangibility, the use of appropriate communication channels to overcome this barrier has become a focal point of research. Recent literature highlights a research interest in travel information sources as a means of improving tourist communications with travel operators. A few attempts have made to increase the research scope of research (e.g. measuring communication effectiveness and marketing communication channels). More studies are needed to advance the understanding of communication mechanisms for systematic and strategic uses.

Figure 1 provides a summary of the diverse developments in travel and tourism marketing research.

Figure 1
Diverse developments in travel and tourism marketing

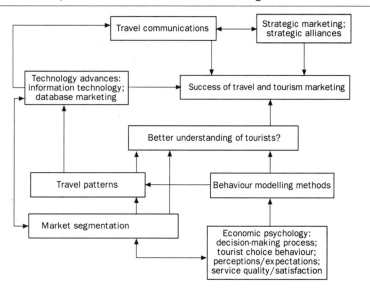

References

(All references are from the *Journal of Travel and Tourism Marketing*)

1 van Raijj, W.F. and Crotts, J.C., "Introduction: the economic psychology of travel and tourism", Vol. 3 No. 3, 1994, pp. 1-20.
2 van Rekom, J., "Adding psychological value to tourism products", Vol. 3 No. 3, 1994, pp. 21-36.
3 Dimanche, F. and Havitz, M.E., "Consumer behaviour and tourism: review and extension of four study areas", Vol. 3 No. 3, 1994, pp. 37-58.
4 Mansfeld, Y., "The 'value stretch' model and its implementation in detecting tourists' class-differentiated destination choice", Vol. 4 No. 3, 1995, pp. 71-92.
5 Costa, P. and Manente, M., "Venice and its visitors: a survey and a model of qualitative choice", Vol. 4 No. 3, 1995, pp. 45-70.
6 Tsaur, S.H. and Tzeng, G.H., "Multiattribute decision making analysis for customer preference of tourist hotels", Vol. 4 No. 4, 1995, pp. 55-70.
7 Moutinho, L. and Curry, B., "Modelling site location decisions in tourism", Vol. 3 No. 2, 1994, pp. 35-59.
8 Hume, W., Pidcock, P. and Johnson, L., "Modelling long distance pleasure travel mode using perceived modal attributes", Vol. 2 No. 1, 1993, pp. 53-68.
9 Seaton, A.V. and Tagg, S., "The family vacation in Europe: paedonomic aspects of choices and satisfactions", Vol. 4 No. 1, 1995, pp. 1-22.
10 Gitelson, R. and Kerstetter, D., "The influence of friends and relatives on travel decision-making", Vol. 3 No. 3, 1994, pp. 59-68.
11 Stewart, S. and Stynes, D.J., "Toward a dynamic model of complex tourism choices: the seasonal home location decision", Vol. 3 No. 3, 1994, pp. 69-88.
12 Madrigal, R., "Parents' perceptions of family members' relative influence in vacation decision making", Vol. 2 No. 4, 1993, pp. 39-58.
13 Ostrowski, R.L., O'Brien, T.V. and Gordon, G.L., "Determinants of service quality in the commercial airline industry: differences between business and leisure travellers", Vol. 3 No. 1, 1994, pp. 19-48.
14 Luk, S.T.K., de Leon, C.T., Leong, F. and Li, E.L.Y., "Value segmentation of tourists' expectations of service quality", Vol. 2 No. 4, 1993, pp. 23-38.
15 Laws, E. and Ryan, C., "Service on flights – issues and analysis by the use of diaries", Vol. 1 No. 3, 1992, pp. 61-72.
16 Johar, J.S. and Sirgy, M.J., "Using segment congruence analysis to determine actionability of travel/tourism segments", Vol. 4 No. 3, 1995, pp. 1-18.
17 Mazanec, J., "Classifying tourists into market segments: a neural network approach", Vol. 1 No. 1, 1992, pp. 39-60.
18 Dimanche, F., Havitz, M.E. and Howard, D.R., "Consumer involvement profiles as a tourism segmentation tool", Vol. 1 No. 4, 1993, pp. 33-52.

Clark Hu
*Diverse developments in
travel and tourism marketing:
a thematic approach*

19 Weaver, P.A., McCleary, K.W. and Jinlin, Z., "Segmenting the business traveler market", Vol. 1 No. 4, 1993, pp. 53-76.

20 Conlin, M.V., "Bermuda tourism: a case study in single segmentation", Vol. 1 No. 4, 1993, pp. 99-112.

21 Davis, B.D., Chappelle, D.E., Sternquist, B.J. and Pysarchik, D.T., "Tourism market segmentation in Michigan's upper peninsula: a regional approach", Vol. 2 No. 1, 1993, pp. 1-30.

22 Lang, C., O'Leary, J.T. and Morrison, A.M., "Activity segmentation of Japanese female overseas travelers", Vol. 2 No. 4, 1993, pp. 1-22.

23 Oppermann, M., "Regional market segmentation analysis in Australia", Vol. 2 No. 4, 1993, pp. 59-74.

24 Wang, Y. and Sheldon, P.J., "The sleeping dragon awakes: the outbound Chinese travel market", Vol. 4 No. 4, 1995, pp. 41-54.

25 Cai, L.A., Hong, G.S. and Morrison, A.M., "Household expenditure patterns for tourism products and services", Vol. 4 No. 4, 1995, pp. 15-40.

26 Roehl, W.S. and Fesenmaier, D.R., "Modelling the influence of information obtained at state welcome centers on visitor expenditures", Vol. 4 No. 3, 1995, pp. 19-28.

27 Opperman, M., "Family life cycle and cohort effects: a study of travel patterns of German residents", Vol. 4 No. 1, 1995, pp. 23-44.

28 Bojanic, D.C., "A look at a modernized family life cycle and overseas travel", Vol. 1 No. 1, 1992, pp. 61-79.

29 Menguc, B., "Major travel agency and trip attributes effective when purchasing a domestic tour from a travel agency: some insights from Istanbul, Turkey", Vol. 3 No. 2, 1994, pp. 1-18.

30 Ross, G.F., "Tourist motivation among backpacker visitors to the wet tropics of Northern Australia", Vol. 1 No. 3, 1992, pp. 43-60.

31 Rutherford, D.O. and Kreck, L.A., "Conventions and tourism: financial add-on or myth? Report of a study in one state", Vol. 3 No. 1, 1994, pp. 49-64.

32 Sheldon, P.J., "Incentive travel: insights into its consumers", Vol. 3 No. 2, 1994, pp. 19-34.

33 Crouch, G.I., "Promotion and demand in international tourism", Vol. 3 No. 3, 1994, pp. 109-35.

34 Covington, B., Thunberg, E.M. and Jauregui, C., "International demand for the United States as a travel destination", Vol. 3 No. 4, 1994, pp. 39-50.

35 Hooper, P., "Evaluation strategies for packaging travel", Vol. 4 No. 2, 1995, pp. 65-82.

36 Luk, S.T.K., Tam, J.L.M. and Wong, S.S.S., "Characteristics of magazine advertisements on hotel service: a content analysis", Vol. 4 No. 3, 1995, pp. 29-44.

37 Uysal, M., Marsinko, A. and Barrett, R.T., "An examination of trip type switching and market share: a Markov chain model application", Vol. 4 No. 1, 1995, pp. 45-56.

38 Gartner, W.C., "Image formation process", Vol. 2 No. 2/3, 1993, pp. 191-216.

39 Schoenbachler, D., di Benedetto, C.A., Gordon, G.L. and Kaminski, P.F., "Destination advertising: assessing effectiveness with the split-run technique", Vol. 4 No. 2, 1995, pp. 1-22.

40 Snepenger, D. and Snepenger, M., "Market structure analysis of media selection practices by travel services", Vol. 2 No. 2/3, 1993, pp. 21-36.

41 Wicks, B.E. and Schuett, M.A., "Using travel brochures to target frequent travellers and 'big-spenders'", Vol. 2 No. 2/3, 1993, pp. 77-90.

42 Duke, C.R. and Persia, M.A., "Effects of distribution channel level on tour purchasing attributes and information sources", Vol. 2 No. 2/3, 1993, pp. 37-56.

43 Selin, S., "Collaborative alliances: new interorganizational forms in tourism", Vol. 2 No. 2/3, 1993, pp. 217-28.

44 McKercher, B., "The destination-market matrix: a tourism market portfolio analysis model", Vol. 4 No. 2, 1995, pp. 23-40.

45 Go, F.M. and Williams, A.P., "Competing and cooperating in the changing tourism channel system", Vol. 2 No. 2/3, 1993, pp. 229-48.

46 Kingsley, I. and Fesenmaier, D.R., "Travel information kiosks: an emerging communications channel for the tourism industry", Vol. 4 No. 1, 1995, pp. 57-70.

47 Deng, S. and Ryan, C., "CRS: tool or determinant of management practice in Canadian travel agents?", Vol. 1 No. 1, 1992, pp. 19-38.

48 Robinson, R. and Keamey, T., "Database marketing for competitive advantage in the airline industry", Vol. 3 No. 1, 1994, pp. 65-82.

49 Reid, L.J. and Reid, S.D., "Communicating tourism supplier services: building repeat visitor relationships", Vol. 2 No. 2/3, 1993, pp. 3-20.

50 Hsieh, S. and O'Leary, J.T., "Communication channels to segment pleasure travelers", Vol. 2 No. 2/3, 1993, pp. 57-76.

51 Noe, F.P., Uysal, M. and Jurowski, C., "Effects of user and trip characteristics on responses to communication messages", Vol. 2 No. 2/3, 1993, pp. 147-70.

52 Fesenmaier, D.R. and Vogt, C.A., "Evaluating the utility of touristic information sources for planning Midwest vacation travel", Vol. 1 No. 2, 1992, pp. 1-18.

53 Goossens, C.F., "External information search: effects of tour brochures with experiential information", Vol. 3 No. 3, 1994, pp. 89-107.

54 Vogt, C.A., Fesenmaier, D.R. and MacKay, K., "Functional and aesthetic information needs underlying the pleasure travel experience", Vol. 2 No. 2/3, 1993, pp. 133-46.

55 Andereck, K.L. and Caldwell, L.L., "The influence of tourists' characteristics on ratings of information sources for an attraction", Vol. 2 No. 2/3, 1993, pp. 171-90.

56 Jurowski, C. and Olsen, M.D., "Scanning the environment of tourism attractions: a content analysis approach", Vol. 4 No. 1, 1995, pp. 71-96.

Perspectives on tourism development

Gavin Eccles
Research Manager (Europe) Worldwide Hospitality and Tourism Trends,
Department of Management Studies, University of Surrey, Guildford, UK
Jorge Costa
Research Manager (Europe) Worldwide Hospitality and Tourism Trends,
Department of Management Studies, University of Surrey, Guildford, UK

Examines aspects of tourism development as reflected by articles published in: *Annals of Tourism Research, Tourism Management* and *Travel and Tourism Analyst* during 1995 (sustainable tourism, transport, new products and the future of tourism) and during the six-year period from 1989-1994 (social trends in tourism, tourism planning and the airline industry).

Introduction

The first part of this article reviews the themes and their related subthemes as reflected in the articles published during 1995 in *Annals of Tourism Research, Tourism Management and Travel and Tourism Analyst.* The themes are reviewed both through tabular and written descriptions. In the second part the same journals are analysed but the summary spans the six-year period from 1989 to 1994. At the end of the article two thematic diagrams relating to 1989-1994 and 1995 respectively are given. These diagrams provide an overview of the main themes, subthemes and proposed actions.

A content analysis of the selected publications revealed a number of themes and the four elaborated here are:
1   sustainable tourism;
2   transport;
3   new products;
4   future of tourism.

Theme 1: sustainable tourism

The main issue arising from Table I is the need to consider sustainability during the early phases of tourism development. Developing a product that sits in harmony with the local environment is addressed in research conducted in Fiji by Ayala[1]. Over the last ten years Fiji has seen a dramatic rise in the number of tourists visiting, from up-market segments right through to the back-packer undertaking a round-the-world trip. Fiji has many differing attractions on offer, and if it is to remain successful, it needs to be integrated with a high-quality product that both considers and fits the local environment. Many Fijians see tourism as a quick way to earn a substantial living, and thus follow the same precedent that was set by Bali some years ago. Ayala therefore concludes that sustainability needs to evolve through effective planning, where guidelines are set on the breadth

and depth of development. Further, locals need to be educated about sustainability in the hope of training people to preserve the product that actually offers them a living.

Research conducted by Harrison[2] and Garcia-Ramon[3] looks at two different countries in their search for a prolonged tourism life cycle. First, Harrison considers Africa, and in particular Swaziland, and reviews progress in the context of life cycles. The author notes that this particular nation underwent rapid growth during the British colonial period but has since declined rapidly. A rejuvenated Swaziland has the potential to develop an excellent tourism product that not only uses the skills of the local people but also fits the local environment. Perhaps by reflecting on examples of badly planned development in Kenya and Tanzania, Swaziland has an opportunity to learn from these and to provide the "perfect destination". Second, Garcia-Ramon[3] looks at Spain, noting that over the past few years Spain has tried desperately to offer products that support the local community. Focusing away from the coastal regions, Garcia-Ramon notes that the rural interior needs to be developed to provide the "ideal" rural tourism product that allows visitors to stay with the local people, so breaking down local-tourist resentment.

Table I reflects a common strand of thinking across the three journals, namely a concern for sustainability. This can be achieved by educating and training people involved in tourism[4] and by the actions of governments and businesses alike in sponsoring initiatives that address the relationship between tourism and the environment[5].

Theme 2: transport

In reviewing the range of articles published across the tourism spectrum (Table II), transportation is notably well presented and especially the activities of airline operators. It is interesting to observe that writers have

Table I
Sustainable tourism

Authors	Focus	Sub-theme
Ayala[1]	To integrate the diversity of Fiji's assets into a high quality eco-product by a combination of planning and conservation and a greater understanding for education	Conservation and ecology
Harrison[2]	The use of the tourism life cycle in developing sustainable tourism in Africa	Sustainable tourism planning and development
Garcia-Ramon[3]	Development of the Spanish tourism industry with a sustainable focus – the need for a new emphasis on promoting the interior, particularly rural tourism	Rural tourism planning
Echtner[4]	The implementation of training programmes to develop sustainable tourism in developing nations	Education and training
Hughes[5]	Help from both governments and businesses in sponsoring initiatives that address the relationship between tourism and the environment	Tourism and environmental relationships
Orams[6]	Defines eco-tourism, and examines how countries adapt their product to address environmentally responsible behaviour	Eco-tourism

focused on European de-regulation, but that in 1995 the emphasis has shifted from scheduled to charter operations. French[7] looks at the future of charters, fighting for slots in a now free and open market. Many airline specialists predicted the end of the charter market owing to legislation imposed from Brussels, but as yet charters are still operating successfully on north European and southern Mediterranean routes. According to French, one reason for this is cost, as people are still prepared to fly late at night on lower priced cheaper charter flights, rather than flying during the day on scheduled services.

Mak and Go[8] note that the airline industry in Asia is suffering as European and US airlines compete for global supremacy. As a result, Asian carriers are forced to negotiate strategic alliances to avoid being sidelined. An area that the Europeans and Americans have not yet entered in their quest for globalization is Africa. According to Endres[9], as broader political stability occurs throughout Africa, growth in its airline industry is anticipated. This may be some way off but greater co-operation within Africa, and between Africa, Europe and the USA would facilitate this development.

In conclusion, these developments are likely to influence tourism, as increases in airline competition will lead to improved service as well as reductions in prices, as operators strive to ensure that capacity targets are met.

Table II
Transport

Authors	Focus	Sub-theme
French[7]	Considers the future for Europe's charter airlines within the full deregulated European airline industry	European airline regulation
Mak and Go[8]	Asian airlines are developing strategic alliances with American and European airlines as they compete for market share	Global airlines
Endres[9]	Greater political stability and the emergence of multinationals in Africa may provide better prospects for the African airline industry	New carriers
Vickerman[10]	Reviews the Channel tunnel's performance in relation to rival carriers, and future prospects, given the tight financial constraints under which it operates	Performance of the Channel tunnel
Peisley[11]	Reviews strategies adopted by the three major operators in the cruise industry in relation to the operating environment of the 1990s	Strategic decisions in the cruise industry

Theme 3: new products

In reviewing tourism products (Table III) one can note that these sometimes have a short life span resulting in a stream of new offerings into the marketplace. During 1995, the USA was seen as being the nation to offer the most varied and differing products, with the most popular being shopping tourism.

Contributions from Finn and Erdem[12] and Timothy and Butler[13] examine the interface between shopping and tourism. A recent surge in the opening of mega-malls in the US, has seen the shopping principle combined with a theme park[12]. The idea behind such a combination is to draw people across state borders, even across continents, in search of a unique experience. As most of these complexes are built outside city centres, one can also see benefits in terms of urban rejuvenation, bringing investment and

job opportunities to the local community. Timothy and Butler[13] examine the reasons for the rising number of Canadian tourists crossing into the USA, especially during 1995. The major reason for a vacation to the USA was in fact to shop. Shopping is referred to as being one of the most enjoyable leisure-time activities, and often tourists spend more money on shopping than other forms of entertainment.

In reviewing the impact of shopping tourism in Europe, there is evidence to suggest that the mega-mall concept is being replicated and we may soon witness people visiting a particular area simply for the shopping experience.

Theme 4: future of tourism

During the course of 1995, a number of published articles (Table IV) speculated on the

Table III
New products

Authors	Focus	Sub-theme
Finn and Erdem[12]	The development of mega-malls as tourist attractions and the combination of shopping and theme parks as an important generator of urban tourism	Developing urban tourism tourism
Timothy and Butler [13]	The recent dramatic increase in the movement of tourists between Canada and the USA and the role of shopping as the generator of this type of tourism	Retailing and tourism
Loverseed[14]	Gaming tourism in North America: a big business as the government relaxes betting laws	Gambling and tourism
Long[15]	New states have been granted access to operate gaming in the USA. Reviews how they are seeking to capitalize on the success of Las Vegas and Atlantic City in attracting tourists	Developing casinos to attract tourists
Nickerson[16]	Can gambling and the development of gaming within the community to help attract tourists to a given area?	The effects of gaming

Table IV
Future of tourism

Authors	Focus	Sub-theme
Towner[17]	Tourism is dominated by Western cultural norms: a change in needed to cater for a wider cross-section of the population	Historical perspectives on tourism
Jefferson[18]	Reviews prospects for tourism over the next ten years, including the impact of older travellers, increased expectations, value for money, quality and environmental issues	The changing nature of tourism
Edgell[19]	Considers tourism as a source of income and employment, which may be enhanced if political red-tape to visiting countries is reduced	Tourism and bureaucracy
Choy[20]	Considers tourism as a way of increasing career opportunities and level of wages for residents working in the industry	Tourism and employment
Ryan[21]	Observes an over supply of graduates from university tourism courses and comments on the inability of the tourist industry to absorb an expanding graduate output	Education and the tourism industry

Gavin Eccles
and Jorge Costa
*Perspectives on tourism
development*

future of tourism and on how the industry may need to adapt and change in order to maintain revenue levels. According to Towner[17] tourism has been dominated by the Western cultural experience where people embark on "tourism journeys", reliving the "grand tour". To overcome this, a closer integration of leisure, recreation and tourism is needed in order to move away from seeing tourism journeys as isolated events.

Elaborating on the future for tourism, Jefferson[18] looks at the prospects for the industry over the next ten years, basing his findings on demographic, socio-economic and political trends. Of major importance demographically is the growth of older travellers. In fact, by the year 2001, one in four Europeans will be over 55, and in the USA and Japan one in seven people will be over 64. The main implication arising from demographic change is likely to be the increased number of senior citizens in the developed countries of the world, those countries that generate tourists. In terms of social trends, one may see increases in the expectations of visitors. A further influential trend arising from Jefferson's study is the amount of holidays people take. Second, third and even fourth holidays are becoming realities, thus helping industry to extend its product's life-cycles.

Another important issue affecting the future of tourism is that of barriers caused by international laws and regulations. Research conducted by Edgell[19] on politics and tourism notes that many countries are using the industry as a generator of income and employment and that these variables could actually be enhanced further if barriers to international tourism can be reduced or eliminated. The European Union has helped to facilitate a diffusion of tourists throughout the 15 member states. Recent signings in the General Agreement on Tariffs and Trade (GATT) may improve the freedom of fair trade in tourism, where positive effects on international tourism growth could be substantial.

Finally, another perspective on how tourism is likely to expand is given in research by Choy[20]. In his work, Choy contends that tourism can be used as a catalyst to increase career opportunities and level of wages for those residents in the countries where tourism is being developed. This situation may lead countries to follow an *ad hoc* approach to development, where little consideration is given for the long-term future and instead, short-term goals of employment and economics are sought. Choy argues that governments must take responsibility for maintaining an economic environment conductive to attracting businesses. This might be

enhanced by private investment in employees' education and by enabling staff to visit a wide array of tourism locations so as to broaden their development experiences.

An analysis of tourism trends from 1989 to 1994

The tourism industry is facing many challenges and many trends. The key concerns currently are sustainability, transport and product development. To elaborate on these points a review of the themes and sub-themes arising from the same journals for the years 1989-1994 is presented.

In terms of commonalities across the three journals (*Annals of Tourism Research, Tourism Management and Travel and Tourism Analyst*) for the six-year period, one can observe that the social trends in tourism, tourism planning and the airline industry are themes covered extensively.

Social trends in tourism
In the context of tourism, the term social trends refers to those products that tourists consume, as well as aspects of destinations that they visit. Throughout the early years of this review many new destinations started to appear on the tourist circuit (Caribbean, Africa and South-east Asia). These destinations had received only a relatively small number of tourists before mass tourism invaded their areas. The relationship between tourists and locals is referred as to hosts' perception, and considers the way locals respond to tourists. According to Dogan[22], hosts have reacted in many differing and varied ways, from complete resistance through to the complete adoption of Western culture. In order to overcome resistance, residents' perceptions need to be carefully considered. According to Ap[23], this is fundamental for tourism planning and development.

The way host communities perceive tourism is strongly influenced by tourists' behaviour, and the power these individuals have over the local community. The number of visitors also affects the way locals relate to tourists; the larger the number the greater the resentment. To overcome this the involvement of local people, or proposals that benefit the whole community, should be adopted.

Tourism planning
Many countries now derive both economic and social benefits from tourism, and use tourism revenues to develop regional infrastructure. For this to be achieved, regional infrastructure needs to be carefully planned

[47]

in order to extend and harness life cycles. One such country which has attempted to develop a tourism industry through a planned system is Poland. According to Kruczala[24], Poland has recently developed a regional policy for tourism taken from their national spatial plan and five-year socio-economic budgets. Further examples from Eastern Europe are cited by Pearlman[25], who notes that Bulgaria has become the most popular destination within the former eastern bloc. Bulgaria's aim in developing tourism has been quite different from the approach taken by Poland, in that the former has not separated tourism and social development. The main task in development has been to try to satisfy the recreational needs of the Bulgarian people through rapid developments in infrastructures.

The developing countries of the world are renowned for implementing tourism as a means of supplementing economic output. Over the period of this review, both Cuba and Nigeria have attempted such an approach. Hinch[26] explains that Cuba is trying to return to former glory by being the most visited island within the Caribbean. To enable this to happen the Cuban government has imposed strict planning controls in an attempt to make tourists feel welcome. African countries are also seeking to use tourism to assist their own economic development efforts. According to Olokesusi[27], Nigeria is seeking to emulate successful projects undertaken in Kenya and Tanzania. A foreseeable problem with this is that Nigeria, like Kenya and Tanzania is attempting to develop game reserves as its primary tourist attraction.

Closely linked to tourism planning, the need for sustainability is one of the most clearly expressed concerns during the period from 1989-1994. Tourism planners are familiar with the problems experienced in Spain, where overdevelopment in the 1970s and early 1980s has led to bad publicity and reductions in tourist numbers. Problems arise when development is rushed, with little consideration for the environment[28]. From the articles reviewed here, it is apparent that successful tourism planning requires both the involvement and participation of residents in the destination areas. There is also a need to develop a product that offers the visitor a real feeling for the local environment, so allowing tourists and locals to interact.

If tourism is to be considered as a source of regional development, planning of local resources and infrastructure is required. In essence, developing countries need to consider this issue, incorporating sustainability

as a means of ensuring long-term success. When planning, governments need to consider the local residents, getting them involved and/or participating in the planning process. It is hoped that this will ensure that projects are supported by the local community.

Airline industry

At present, Europe is witnessing airline de-regulation imposed by the European Union, where the intent is to free up slots on all intra-European routes. The airline companies are working very hard to develop their infrastructure and route networks to take advantage of this situation. Wheatcroft[29] notes that the introduction of a single European airline market will accelerate the trend towards multinational ownership. Thus, in order for fair competition to flourish, Marshall[30] notes that Europe's airports need to be developed to enable them to handle an increase in flights. Further, French[31] predicts that the movement away from governmental control of state airlines is a critical issue. Will this allow international competitive oligopoly to develop?

In essence, many small European carriers will be swallowed up by the stronger, existing privatized European airlines. If this is the case the consumer will have fewer airlines to choose from, the exact situation that has occurred in the USA. As airlines continue to strive for European dominance, the Asian carriers are seeking to link into the European network, and, to gain access, require strategic alliances, in particular with those carriers that are currently looking to control European aviation.

If not contained, European airline de-regulation is likely to determine the development of a small group of global mega-airlines.

Conclusion

During the seven years, 1989-1995 inclusive, many aspects of the tourism industry have changed as political, economic and social changes have occurred in both the receiving and generating countries. Politically, it was only seven years ago that Europe witnessed the interaction of East and West. In the period of this review, both Prague (Czech Republic) and Budapest (Hungary) became the fastest growing short-break holiday destinations. Florida and Kenya were seen as being the "in-resorts' at the start of the 1990s, as people wanted to extend their travel experiences. Predictions for 1997 and beyond are showing increases in tourist numbers to Turkey. The economic conditions have deeply affected the tourism industry through exchange rate

Gavin Eccles
and Jorge Costa
*Perspectives on tourism
development*

fluctuations and recessionary periods. These two issues contribute to lower disposable incomes referred to as being a major determinant in deciding whether people take a holiday. It is interesting to note that within the journals reviewed here, little has been written on the political and economic implications for tourism.

In reviewing the main trends identified during the period from 1989 to 1995 the following concluding observations are presented:
• Sustainability can be seen as a fundamental requirement for countries attempting to

develop their tourism industry. In the process of developing a tourism product, planners must ensure harmony with the local environment. Sustainability needs to evolve through effective planning with clear guidelines on the breadth and depth of the development. This goal can be achieved by educating and training people involved with tourism and by the actions of governments and organizations in sponsoring initiatives that address the relationship between tourism and the environment.

Figure 1
Summary of main themes and sub-themes – 1995

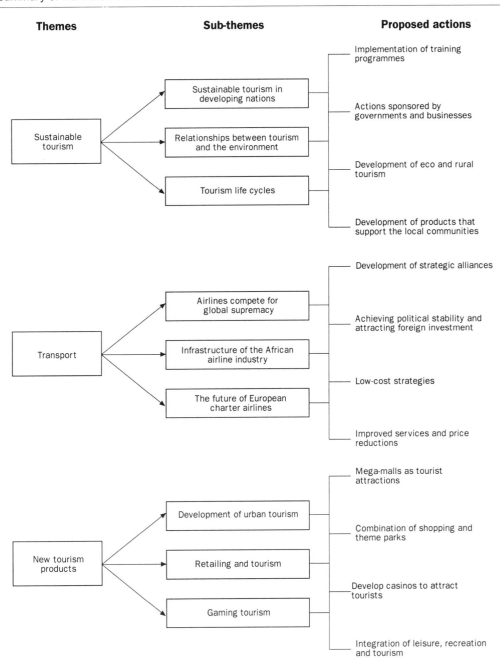

Gavin Eccles
and Jorge Costa
*Perspectives on tourism
development*

• Transport has been a theme extensively covered in the tourism literature, where special emphasis lies with the airline industry. Here, the impact of deregulation on the European charter market can be seen as an area that may cause concern. In a different geographic setting Asian carriers are being required to negotiate strategic alliances with European and American airlines, mainly in their strive for globalization.
• The USA has witnessed a recent surge in mega-malls that combine shopping with a theme park experience. This encourages a greater array of tourists to visit the location. Further, the location of such complexes outside city centres may help urban rejuvenation.
• The future development of tourism has been the subject of recent speculation. Growth in the number of older people travelling, the number of holidays taken and the high expectations of tourists are seen as examples of trends that are shaping the industry.

Summaries of the main themes and sub-themes are presented in Figures 1 and 2.

Figure 2
Summary of main themes and sub-themes – 1989-1994

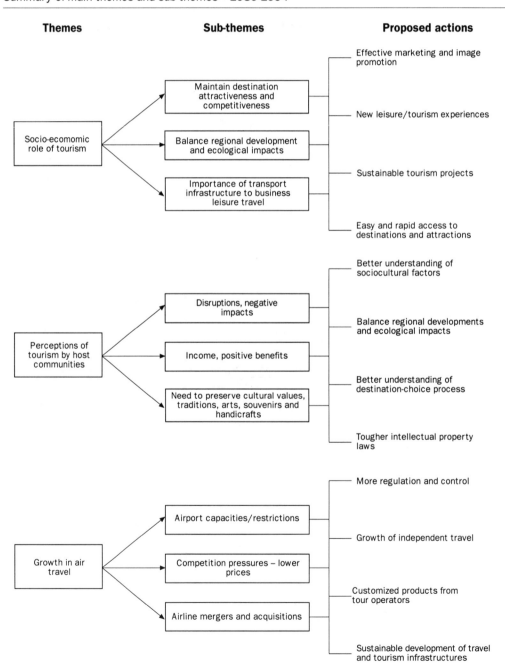

Gavin Eccles
and Jorge Costa
*Perspectives on tourism
development*

References

1 Ayala, H., "From quality product to eco product: will Fiji set a precedent", *Tourism Management*, Vol. 16 No. 1, 1995, pp. 39-47.

2 Harrison, D., "Development of tourism in Swaziland", *Annals of Tourism Research*, Vol. 22 No. 1, 1995, pp. 135-56.

3 Garcia-Ramon, M.D., "Farm tourism, gender and the environment in Spain", *Annals of Tourism Research*, Vol. 22 No. 2, 1995, pp. 267-82.

4 Echtner, C.M., "Entrepreneurial training in developing countries", *Annals of Tourism Research*, Vol. 22 No. 1, 1995, pp. 119-34.

5 Hughes, G., :"The cultural construction of sustainable tourism", *Tourism Management*, Vol. 16 No. 1, 1995, pp. 49-59.

6 Orams, M.B., "Towards a more desirable form of ecotourism", *Tourism Management*, Vol. 16 No. 1, 1995, pp. 3-8.

7 French, T., "Transport: charter airlines in Europe", *Travel and Tourism Analyst*, No. 4, 1995, pp. 4-19.

8 Mak, B. and Go, F., "Matching global competition: co-operation among Asian airlines", *Tourism Management*, Vol. 16 No. 1, 1995, pp. 61-5.

9 Endres, G., "Transport: airlines in sub-Saharan Africa", *Travel and Tourism Analyst*, No. 5, 1995, pp. 4-23.

10 Vickerman, R., "Transport: the channel tunnel – a progress report", *Travel and Tourism Analyst*, No. 3, 1995, pp. 4-20.

11 Peisley, T., "Transport: the cruise ship industry to the 21st century", *Travel and Tourism Analyst*, No. 2, 1995, pp. 4-25.

12 Finn, A. and Erdem, T., "The economic impact of a mega-multi-mall. Estimation issues in the case of West Edmonton Mall", *Tourism Management*, Vol. 16 No. 5, 1995, pp. 367-73.

13 Timothy, D.J. and Butler, R.W., "Cross-border shopping: a North American perspective", *Annals of Tourism Research*, Vol. 22 No. 1, 1995, pp. 16-34.

14 Loverseed, H., "Market segments: gambling tourism in North America", *Travel and Tourism Analyst*, No. 3, 1995, pp. 40-53.

15 Long, P.T., "Casino gaming in the United States: 1994 status and implications", *Tourism Management*, Vol. 16 No. 3, 1995, pp. 198-97.

16 Nickerson, N., "Tourism and gambling content analysis", *Annals of Tourism Research*, Vol. 22 No. 1, 1995, pp. 53-66.

17 Towner, J., "What is tourism's history", *Tourism Management*, Vol. 16 No. 5, 1995, pp. 339-43.

18 Jefferson, A., "Prospects for tourism – a practitioners view", *Tourism Management*, Vol. 16 No. 2, 1995, pp. 101-5.

19 Edgell, D.L., "A barrier-free future for tourism", *Tourism Management*, Vol. 16 No. 2, 1995, pp. 107-10.

20 Choy, D.J.L., "The quality of tourism employment", *Tourism Management*, Vol. 16 No. 2, 1995, pp. 129-37.

21 Ryan, C., "Tourism courses: a new concern for a new time", *Tourism Management*, Vol. 16 No. 3, 1995, pp. 97-100.

22 Dogan, H., "Forms of adjustment: sociocultural impacts of tourism", *Annals of Tourism Research*, Vol. 16 No. 2, 1989, pp. 216-36.

23 Ap, J., "Residents' perceptions on tourism impacts", *Annals of Tourism Research*, Vol. 19 No. 4, 1992, pp. 665-90.

24 Kruczala, J., "Tourism planning in Poland", *Annals of Tourism Research*, Vol. 17 No. 1, 1990, pp. 69-78.

25 Pearlman, M., "Conflicts and constraints in Bulgaria's tourism sector", *Annals of Tourism Research*, Vol. 17 No. 1, 1990, pp. 103-22.

26 Hinch, T.D., "Cuban tourism industry. Its re-emergence and future", *Tourism Management*, Vol. 11 No. 3, 1990, pp. 214-16.

27 Olokesusi, F., "Developing the game reserves in Nigeria, in order to help improve the country's employment", *Tourism Management*, Vol. 11 No. 2, 1990, pp. 153-62.

28 May, V., "Tourism, environment and development. Values, sustainability and stewardship", *Tourism Management*, Vol. 12 No. 2, 1991, pp. 112-18.

29 Wheatcroft, S., "Current trends in aviation", *Tourism Management*, Vol. 10 No. 3, 1989, pp. 213-17.

30 Marshall, C., "Practical solutions to European air traffic congestion", *Travel and Tourism Analyst*, No. 4, 1990, pp. 64-73.

31 French, T., "The US and European airline commissions", *Travel and Tourism Analyst*, No. 6, 1993, pp. 14-18.

Challenges for hospitality and tourism operators: a North American perspective

Sridhar Prabhu
Research Manager (N. America) Worldwide Hospitality and Tourism Trends,
William F. Harrah College of Hotel Administration, University of Nevada,
Las Vegas, USA

Identifies five main themes from the articles published in the *Cornell Hotel and Restaurant Administration Quarterly* during a five-year review period from 1990-1995. The theme areas (hospitality training and education, human resources and organizations, restaurant and food service operations, hotel operations and development and travel and tourism management) serve to identify some of the main challenges that hospitality and tourism operators are currently facing.

Introduction

The purpose of this review is to identify the key hospitality and tourism themes as reflected by articles published in the *Cornell Hotel and Restaurant Administration Quarterly* during the years 1990-1995, the years included in the Worldwide Hospitality and Tourism Trends database. *Cornell Quarterly* is a premier publication geared towards hospitality executives, managers and consultants in the lodging, resort and food service sector, as well as academics and students in business and hotel and restaurant management schools.

This review identifies five prominent themes, each with related sub-themes, which are intended to reflect the major issues and trends arising during the review period. These themes are presented in tabular format listing the author(s), sub-theme and the focus of the research, and are accompanied by a written discussion of the major issues. The five theme areas include:

1 hospitality training and education;
2 human resources and organizations;
3 restaurant and food service operations;
4 hotel operations and development; and
5 travel and tourism management.

Hospitality training and education

The sub-themes in Table I focus on the following issues: employee training programmes and management development; hospitality education and job expectations; and technology in training and education.

Employee training programmes and management development

Haywood[1] suggests that the most effective training programmes are ones that convey information and demand measurable performance improvements that match predetermined goals. His research indicates that firms committed to increasing effectiveness and competitiveness have an organizational environment that allows employees to function at their best. However, Conrade *et al.*[2] found in their research that many lodging companies in the USA do not offer planned,

quality employee-training activities and spend much less than non-hospitality businesses on such training programmes.

Shaw and Patterson[3] describe what Canadian hospitality managers look for in external management-development programmes, including those subject areas that require more education and training. Their research reveals that the highest-rated subject areas include service quality, motivation and training, and communication skills. The least-rated subjects include the areas of advertising, personal selling, and research methods. Marketing topics are rated higher overall by lodging managers than by food-service managers, while each rated accounting, finance, and ethics in the mid-range.

Hospitality education and job expectations

Goodman and Sprague[4] report that, owing to the expanding role of services in the world economy, business schools have begun to address the needs of service operations. Concurrently, many hospitality education programmes have begun to deviate from a strict hospitality management orientation towards a more general business orientation. The authors suggest that, in order to serve the needs of both students and industry adequately, hospitality schools must redirect their orientation towards the needs of the hospitality industry. Clark and Arbel[6] emphasize the need to globalize the student bodies in hospitality schools in order to keep pace with the international nature of the hospitality industry. They recommend that hospitality schools intensify their efforts to accept more international students, require more international faculty members, and to develop programmes that serve the needs of the global community. In another study, Evans[5] reports that universities are beginning to develop more hospitality graduate programmes to address the need to develop top managers and educators. The author explains that ideal graduate programmes require students to have competencies based in industry, on functional management skills, and on research.

Durocher and Goodman[7] point out that training programme expectations which graduates have of industry are not indicative of the actual experiences they receive. They describe discrepancies in length of programme, hours required, specializations to be learned, and after-training expectations such as pay-rises and relocation assistance. The authors suggest that better communication is needed between companies and schools, and that educators should encourage students to examine a wide range of opportunities before accepting a job offer.

Technology in training and education

Durocher[8] describes the major drawbacks of the two most prevalent training methods used currently in the hospitality industry. He criticizes the "buddy system", in which one employee trains another, saying that it often leads to the amassing of bad habits. Also, he points out the inefficiency of using managers to handle training since they may be leaving their other essential duties unattended. Thus, the author suggests the use of interactive videodiscs to allow new employees to see, hear, and react to typical situations faced on the job. He explains that the interactive training programme can also be used to test the trainees' knowledge, explain areas of ignorance, and strengthen deficient areas. Similarly, Harris and West[9] describe how a few hospitality-education schools are successfully using interactive technologies to train students in front-desk operations, marketing strategy, and other areas relating to the hospitality industry. The authors suggest that the most successful training programmes combine multimedia training with peer-group sessions, supervisor training, and take-home lessons from textbooks and workbooks.

Table I
Hospitality training and education

Authors	Focus	Sub-theme
Haywood[1]	Develops an eight-point model for effective training by analysing two successful training programmes. The aim is to determine what constitutes an effective training programme	Effective training programmes
Conrade *et al.*[2]	Compares the perceptions of corporate and property level lodging personnel on the value of training and its industry-wide implementation	Training in hotels
Shaw and Patterson[3]	Surveys Canadian hospitality managers to determine what they look for in external management-development programmes, including subject areas that need more education and training programmes	Management development programmes
Goodman and Sprague[4]	Examines current hospitality-education programmes to determine if they are serving the needs of the students and the industry. Identifies problem areas and gives possible solutions	Hospitality education
Evans[5]	Considers the role of graduate programmes in hospitality education and proposes what should constitute an ideal graduate programme, including student requirements and programme objectives	Graduate hospitality education
Clark and Arbel[6]	Examines the need to globalize the student bodies in hospitality education schools. Identifies ways to globalize student bodies and faculty as well	Globalizing hospitality education
Durocher and Goodman[7]	Considers reasons why the expectations that graduates have of the industry's training programmes do not necessarily match the reality	Training programme expectations
Durocher[8]	Describes how interactive video discs can be used as a method to handle employee training. Explains why normal training methods have drawbacks	Using interactive video discs in training
Harris and West [9]	Describes the use of computer-based multimedia presentations in hospitality education training. Examines studies indicating increased efficiency and learner motivation using multimedia training	Using multimedia in hospitality education training

Human resources and organizations

The sub-themes of Table II focus on the following human resource and organizational issues: employee empowerment and motivation; employee turnover, selection and termination; work environment and organizational climate; and legal issues of employment.

Employee empowerment and motivation

Employee empowerment requires management to give up control, without giving up accountability, and to trust subordinates with the authority to make decisions. Sternberg[10] argues that hotels can increase operational efficiency, employee productivity and guest satisfaction through empowerment. The author cites examples of how empowerment has worked to benefit hospitality operations.

A study conducted by Simon and Enz[11] among 278 workers at 12 hotels in the USA and Canada reports that the three most important job motivation factors for hotel employees are: good wages; job security; and

Table II
Human resources and organizations

Authors	Focus	Sub-theme
Sternberg[10]	Reports on how hotels can use employee empowerment to improve operational efficiency, increase employee productivity and guest satisfaction. Discusses examples of how empowerment has worked to benefit hospitality operations	Employee empowerment
Simons and Enz[11]	A survey of 278 workers at 12 hotels in the USA and Canada reveals hotel employee motivation factors. Identifies these motivation factors overall, by age, and by department	Employee motivation
Hogan[12]	Examines how five hotel organizations with different managerial styles handle employee turnover. Offers recommendations on how to reduce turnover	Employee turnover
Kennedy and Berger[13]	Argues that a contributing factor to employee turnover in hotels is the one-dimensional focus of their orientation programmes. Recommends ways to increase effectiveness of orientation programmes	Newcomer socialization
Murthy and Murrman[14]	Discusses how hospitality firms can use employee leasing as a strategy for dealing with turnover, absenteeism, training, and other associated costs of employment. Outlines the advantages and concerns of employee leasing	Employee leasing
Vallen[15]	Examines the relationship of organizational structure and burnout in the hospitality industry. Discusses techniques to use to increase job satisfaction	Organizational climate and job satisfaction
Tabacchi et al.[16]	Examines the high level of burnout among middle-level managers in food-service outlets. Reviews methods to reduce manager burnout	Managerial burnout
Hamilton et al.[17]	Discusses the new definition of sexual harassment that includes environmental factors. Reviews court rulings and current expectations of victims and management in sexual harassment claims	Hostile work environment
Sherry[18]	Examines employer liability for sexual harassment by managers. Discusses court rulings on responsibility in such cases	Sexual harassment
Woods and Kavanaugh[19]	Reports on the issues and implications of the Americans with Disabilities Act (ADA). Focuses on how the ADA affects workers, employers, and the public	Americans with Disabilities Act
Pellissier[20]	Discusses how management should structure disciplinary procedures to allow for a proper termination of an employee. Reviews the legal issues surrounding the termination process	Termination procedures

Sridhar Prabhu
*Challenges for hospitality and
tourism operators: a North
American perspective*

opportunities for advancement and development. However, while all respondents rated
"good wages" as their most important job
priority, the study found differences among
hotel workers based on their age and department.

Employee turnover, selection and termination

Hogan[12] examines how five organizations
with different managerial styles handle
employee turnover. Based on his results, the
companies emphasized the following in vary-
ing degrees: ongoing training and education,
employee empowerment, open communication with management, and appreciation for
accomplishment. Kennedy and Berger[13]
describe how a contributing factor to
employee turnover in hotels is the one-dimen-
sional informational focus of their orientation programme. They report that the orientation programmes at hotels are not paying
much attention to the emotional needs of
their employees, such as the anxiety of being
newly engaged. The authors recommend that
orientation programmes that deal with both
the emotional and the informational needs of
new employees will contribute to reduced
turnover. Murthy and Murrman[14] argue
that employee leasing offers hospitality firms
a strategy for dealing with turnover, absenteeism, training, unemployment costs, and
other associated costs. The authors report
that leasing generally secures improved benefits and opportunity for advancement for
employees.

Pellissier[20] discusses how to structure
disciplinary procedures to meet the requirements of proper employee termination. The
author reports that, in order to end an
employment relationship legally, the
employer must set specific requirements,
show that the employee is aware of the
requirements, establish progressive disciplinary steps, and give the employee written
warnings that continued misbehaviour will
lead to termination.

Work environment and organizational climate

A study conducted by Vallen[15] found that
there is a high correlation between employee
burnout and organizational structure. Specifically, he reports that employees in highly
participative organizations, in terms of supportive managerial relationships, group
decision making, and team goals,
experienced less burnout. On the other hand,
his study found that organizations with auto-
cratic decision making, employee mistrust,
and tight control experienced far greater
burnout. The author suggests that job

satisfaction can be enhanced when positive,
supportive relationships are developed.
Tabacchi *et al.*[16] report that the highest
levels of burnout in the hotel sector are found
among middle-level managers in food-service
outlets, since they face the pressures of
employees' demands on one side and the
supervisors' on the other. They agree with the
previous assessment that the difference
between a functioning manager and a
burned-out employee is the amount and type
of support the person receives on the job.

Legal issues of employment

Woods and Kavanaugh[19] report on the
issues and implications of the Americans
with Disabilities Act (ADA). The major provision of the act requires employers to make
"reasonable" adjustments in the workplace to
accommodate disabled workers. The authors
give suggestions on how to prepare for the
ADA, including how to implement training
programmes to educate managers on dealing
with disabled workers.

Hamilton *et al.*[17] report that recent legal
proceedings have redefined sexual harassment via a "hostile work environment" rul-
ing. The new rulings define sexual harassment as experienced by anyone who feels
they are receiving unwanted attention.
Sherry[18] reports that the US Supreme
Court mandates that employers respond for
the wrongful acts of managers when such
acts occur within the scope of the managers'
employment.

Restaurant and food-service operations

The sub-themes in Table III provide an
insight into the trends in restaurant and foodservice operations during the review period.
The sub-themes range from issues concerning marketing strategy and segmentation,
restaurant development and technology, and
customer service and satisfaction.

Market strategy and segmentation

Panyko[21] reports on the two major marketing challenges faced by food-service operators
in the 1990s. First, he examines the continuous need to focus on the large "baby boomer"
group of middle-agers. Second, he refers to
the challenge of marketing to the groups on
the far ends of the population spectrum –
young people and people 50 years old or over.
However, regardless of age, the author indicates that the focus of marketing should be
based on the premiss that consumers purchase food according to their desires for
health, style, expression, and use of time.

Table III
Restaurant and food service operations

Authors	Focus	Sub-theme
Panyko[21]	Discusses the marketing challenges food-service marketers face in the 1990s. Includes specific discussion on market segmentation	Food service marketing
Muller and Woods[22]	Reviews the restaurant industry explaining the attributes of five separate restaurant segments from the point of view of management and customers	Market segmentation
Carmin and Norkus[23]	Explores the concept of psychological pricing and its effect on consumer purchasing behaviour	Pricing strategies
Goldman and Eyster [24]	Discusses hotel food and beverage leases from the restaurant operators' viewpoint. Reviews common lease provisions of which restaurant operators should be wary	Hotel F&B leases
Paul [25]	Examines the emergence of the chain restaurant industry. Discusses factors contributing to its growth	Trends in the chain restaurant industry
Shriber et al. [26]	Investigates correlation between changes in population and restaurant growth. Describes procedure for the application of the technique	Population changes and restaurant success
Muller and Inman[27]	Examines how the combination of demographic and geographic information can be applied to identifying ideal restaurant locations	Geodemographics of restaurant development
Dube et al.[28]	Studies seven service-quality attributes to determine their significance on customers' intent to return	Customer satisfaction and repeat business
Stevens et al.[29]	Proposes "DINESERV", 29-item questionnaire, as a tool to determine how customers view a restaurant's quality, and to determine customers' expectations	Measuring service quality
Kasanava[30]	Discusses the impact of computers in multiunit food-service operations. Reviews specific computer applications for specific multiunit restaurant formats	Computers and multiunit food-service operations
Kasanava[31]	Reports on PC-based registers and their impact on the transaction-processing marketplace. Discusses current and possible future uses of the technology	Point-of-sale technology

Muller and Woods[22] examine the trend of the expansion of the typical three-segment restaurant typology of quick service, midscale, and upscale to include moderate upscale and business dining. The authors' examination of the different segments' attributes shows why quick-service restaurants are putting considerable pressure on midscale operations, and why even some upscale restaurants are susceptible to competition from chains. In a similar study, Paul[25] recounts the emergence of chain restaurants as the dominant force in the restaurant sector. The author reports that a large portion of the industry's growth has come from the advent of major quick-chain restaurants. He attributes this growth to such factors as the rise of two-income households and the chain restaurants' competitive advantages in market concentration and advertising.

Carmin and Norkus[23] explore the concept of psychological pricing, which normally involves using a "0", "9", or "5" at the end of an item's price. The authors' study indicates that there is a definite change in consumer purchase behaviour when using odd cents pricing in a price-sensitive market. The authors also suggest that factors such as price differences between the highest and lowest priced menu items and perceived quality as conveyed by menu prices are important considerations.

Restaurant development and technology
Goldman and Eyster[24] identify a trend for a hotel's food and beverage (F&B) operations to be managed by an independent operator or restaurant company under a management contract or lease. The authors report that such arrangements reduce the economic and marketplace obstacles connected with new operations. The authors also review common lease provisions of which restaurant operators should be wary.

Kasanava[30] reports on how computers have changed the nature of multiunit food-service operations, both at the unit and corporate levels, and how food-service chains are adopting computer networks at an unprecedented rate. Kasanava[31], in another study, points out that as vendors begin to transfer applications to more flexible platforms, the transaction-processing marketplace in restaurants will be dominated by PC-based registers (PCRs).

A study by Shriber *et al.*[26] provides time-series data regarding how restaurants have fared in the USA. By comparing these data to changes in population by region, the author attempts to determine where opportunities exist and where markets are saturated. An interesting fact from the study reveals that changes in population do not necessarily lead to corresponding changes in restaurant sales. In a similar study, Muller and Inman[27] explain how a combination of demographic and geographic information can be applied to identifying locations for restaurant units.

Customer service and satisfaction

Customer satisfaction is perhaps the best indicator of repeat business, the foundation for most restaurants' success. Dube *et al.*[28] conducted a study of seven service-quality attributes and found that all seven are significant contributors to repeat business. The authors recommend that although it seems appropriate to improve on attributes characterized as significant weaknesses, it is up to management to perform a cost-benefit analysis to see if making changes will improve customer satisfaction and increase repeat business. Similarly, Stevens *et al.*[29] describe how "DINESERV", a service-quality questionnaire, can be used as a reliable source for determining how consumers view a restaurant's quality. The authors explain that "DINESERV" is used to measure consumers' expectations and allows the restaurant operator to get the customers' viewpoint on the restaurant's quality, and to identify problem areas that need resolving.

Hotel operations and development

The sub-themes of Table IV fall under the headings of marketing strategy and segmentation, customer service and satisfaction, and technological innovations.

Marketing strategy and segmentation

Hotels use many different kinds of segmentation strategy. Mehta and Vera[32] describe a five-star hotel in Singapore that has divided its market into eight segments, including individual, corporate, airline crews, and group tours. Comparing this segmentation strategy to other commonly used schemes, the authors found that the hotel's segmentation strategy method worked effectively to separate the segments on the basis of how they choose and evaluate hotels before and after their stay. Furthermore, the study indicates that such segmentation strategies based on income and nationality are weak, while purpose of travel is an effective basis for segmentation.

Hanks *et al.*[33] report on a new pricing strategy used by firms such as Marriott that help hotels maximize revenue by offering different room products to different market segments. The author states that the key to this approach is to segment the markets and keep them segmented. For example, Marriott has set up "fenced rates" discounts for its leisure travellers, that tie them to certain restrictions such as advanced purchase and no refund. The author suggests that this pricing strategy discourages high-rate segments from attempting to trade down because of the restrictions.

A study done by Toh and Rivers[34] suggests that frequent-guest programmes (FGP) have little effect on most travellers' hotel choice. For those who are aware of such programmes, reasons cited for lack of use include loss of flexibility in selecting hotels, too few trips to earn anything, and unattractive rewards. However, frequent guest programmes may be important to a select group of travellers. McCleary and Weaver[35] note that business travellers may be willing to pay more to earn FGP benefits. The authors recommend that, because of the possible size of the segment which may be influenced by FGP programmes, it is risky for hotel chains to drop their FGP programmes unless the entire industry does so.

Customer service and satisfaction

Lewis and Nightingale[36] argue that focusing on service is different from focusing on the customer. They suggest that service be defined relative to customers' needs, and the price of a room reflect the guests' expectations as to the desired level of service. In another study, Barsky and Labagh[37] describe how Western hotels can emulate the service standards of Asian hotels with some additional employee training and some changes in operating procedures.

Technological innovations

Emmer *et al.*[38] report on a trend involving travel agents booking hotel rooms electronically via global distribution systems (GDS). The authors state that the key for travel

Table IV
Hotel operations and development

Authors	Focus	Sub-theme
Mehta and Vera[32]	Describes the unique segmentation strategy of a five-star hotel in Singapore. Compares the strategy's effectiveness to other common segmentation schemes	Segmentation strategy
Hanks *et al.*[33]	Reviews a new approach to hotel discounting, which establishes discrete rate tiers for different segments. Describes Marriott's attempt at this discounting approach	Discounting in the hotel industry
Toh and Rivers[34]	Describes the use of frequent guest programmes (FGP) among travellers. Cites reasons for FGP's ineffectiveness and offers suggestions on how to improve the programme	Frequent guest programmes
McCleary and Weaver[35]	Reports on the effectiveness of frequent guest programmes and describes its usage patterns among various travel segments	Frequent guest programmes
Lewis and Nightingale[36]	Identifies differences between focusing on service and focusing on the customer. Suggests ways to develop a sound customer service strategy	Customer service
Barsky and Labagh[37]	Introduces a straightforward way to assess a hotel's current situation with respect to customer satisfaction and shows how to use this approach to improve planning and decision making	Customer satisfaction
Emmer *et al.*[38]	Reports on the trend of marketing hotels using global distribution systems(GDS). Cites potential benefits of GDS and provides guidelines for its use in the hotel and travel sectors	Marketing hotels using global distribution systems
Reid and Sandler[39]	Examines a study of 35 top lodging companies and their adoption of technological innovation. Reports on usage of these innovations, and their effect on the level of customer service	Technological innovations
Warren and Ostergren[40]	Outlines challenges faced by hotel marketers in the 1990s. Reviews the role of computer technology to handle marketing and advertising, and improve customer service	Role of technology in marketing

agents to rely on GDS listings is to make sure that the rates offered electronically are complete, accurate, and the lowest available. Reid and Sandler[39] describe other lodging trends involving technology including electronic door locks, computer modems, in-room VCRs, and in-room fax machines. The authors report that offering such innovations to save money or for the guests' benefit tends to improve the general level of service within the lodging industry as a whole. Another technological trend is noted by Warren and Ostergren[40] who report that with the advent of computer technology, hotel marketers can engage in micro-marketing, where you can use databases to capture vast information on customers and market directly to their needs.

Travel and tourism management

The sub-themes in Table V come under the headings of marketing strategy and segmentation, disaster planning, and sustainable tourism.

Marketing strategy and segmentation

Using Singapore as an example of a destination, Mehta *et al.*[41] explore the complexities of attracting the incentive-travel market. The authors assessment is that selling travel packages to corporations who in turn use them to reward employees is more profitable, when properly done, than the meetings business. The authors recommend that providing a desirable destination, being creative, and offering unique programmes are the keys to attracting first-time incentive customers. Also, delivering flawless customer service, well-trained employees, and follow-up calls are said to be keys to ensuring repeat business. Similarly, Sorensen[42] reports that adventure travellers constitute a relatively small but growing market segment. Adventure travel normally comprises small groups who go to a

Sridhar Prabhu
*Challenges for hospitality and
tourism operators: a North
American perspective*

Table V
Travel and tourism management

Authors	Focus	Sub-theme
Mehta *et al.*[41]	Explores the complexities of attracting the incentive travel market, using Singapore as an example of a destination. Describes techniques used in promoting incentive travel	Incentive travel marketing
Sorensen[42]	Reports on the special-interest travel market of adventure travellers. Examines opportunities for hotels to market to this segment	Special-interest travel market
Manning and Dougherty[45]	Describes need for the public and private sectors to collaborate to ensure that tourism does not exceed capacity. Reviews the role of an ecosystem approach to travel planning	Sustaining tourism
Iwanowski and Rushmore[46]	Explains why lodging operators should incorporate environmental programmes into each level of their operation. Reviews existing systems and operations	Environmental programmes
Durocher[43]	Examines tourism recovery after a natural disaster. Reviews critical lessons learned from the Hurricane Ininki disaster in Hawaii	Recovery marketing
Drabek [44]	Reports on disaster planning and response by tourism business executives. Examines the roles of the host community and their decision-making processes in dealing with disasters	Disaster planning
Khan *et al.*[47]	Explores the relationship between tourist spending and its effect on a nation's economy. Examines the multiplier effect on Singapore's tourism industry	Economic impact of tourism

specific destination for a specific reason. The author assesses that the agents who package adventure travel do not normally deal with major hotel chains. Sorensen claims that this is a unique opportunity for hotels since adventure travellers are generally affluent and travel often.

Disaster planning
Durocher[43] states that tourism recovery after a natural disaster depends on the extent of damages, the efficiency with which facilities are brought back online, and the effectiveness of marketing to advertise the destination's status. Unfortunately, hospitality executives begin planning for disaster after it has occurred, as found by a study by Drabek[44]. The authors point out that it makes good business sense to be environmentally conscious, in that it is ultimately profitable and it promotes the firm as being a good neighbour and corporate citizen.

Sustainable tourism
Manning and Dougherty[45] report that to prevent environmental or cultural damage that curtails tourism, operators and planners need to co-operate with governmental authorities and managers in other industries to plan strategies to ensure that tourism to a locale does not exceed the capacity of that

destination. The authors describe an environmental impact assessment (EIA) as a method for determining that capacity. They recommend that an EIA should take into account the relationship between demand from travellers and the sensitive environmental characteristics of the site. In a similar study, Iwanowski and Rushmore[46] explain why lodging companies should incorporate environmental programmes into each level of their operation. The authors present specific tactics and ideas that illustrate how to implement programmes concerning solid-waste management, water conservation, and energy management.

Conclusion
The basis for this review was to identify the prominent themes emerging in the hospitality and tourism industries during the period 1990-1995, as reflected by articles in the *Cornell Hotel and Restaurant Administration Quarterly*. From the themes identified, it is possible to identify distinct problem areas and challenging areas of opportunites for the hospitality industry, and in conclusion, these are summarized below:
• In order for hospitality students to correctly gauge their job expectations, better

Table VI

Trends in the hospitality and tourism industries: a North American perspective. Themes, subthemes and observations based on a review of 335 entries (1990-1995) in the *Cornell Hotel and Restaurant Administration Quarterly*

Authors	Focus	Sub-theme
Theme 1: **hospitality training and education**	Value of training in the lodging industry; effective training models; management development programmes in Canada; trends in hospitality education; training programme expectations; technology in education and training	In order for hospitality students and management trainees to gauge their job expectations correctly, better communication is needed among educators and industry professionals in the hospitality industry. Hospitality education needs to refocus on serving the needs of the hospitality industry, as well as the global community. The industry needs to provide more quality training programmes, which may involve taking advantage of interactive training methods to go along with supervised training.
Theme 2: **human resources and organizations**	Employee empowerment and motivation; employee turnover; employee leasing; organizational climate and job satisfaction; managerial burnout; sexual harassment; Americans with Disabilities Act	There is a need for hospitality organizations to increase employee motivation through involvement. Empowerment is cited as a key to increasing employee motivation, reducing turnover, and improving productivity. To handle employee turnover and burnout, management also needs to focus on providing a supportive organizational environment. Finally, management be cognizant on how to deal with legal matters pertaining to employment, including the employee disability and sexual harassment rulings
Theme 3: **restaurant and food service operations**	Food service marketing; market segmentation and pricing strategies; hotel F&B leases; trends in the chain restaurant industry; locational analysis; customer satisfaction and repeat business; measuring service quality; technological innovations in food service operations	The quick-service chain restaurant sector is becoming the dominant force in the restaurant business owing to their ability to satisfy a myriad of customer needs. Methods are continuously being used and developed by the industry to measure consumers' expectations in relation to satisfaction. The restaurant sector needs to use these methods, along with proper employee training, operating procedures, and technological innovations to enhance overall customer service and satisfaction
Theme 4: **hotel operations and development**	Segmentation and pricing strategies for hotels; frequent guest programmes; customer service and satisfaction; technological innovations in the hotel industry	Technological innovations are and will continue to be a critical part of the hotel sector. Technology not only helps increase operational efficiency, but contributes to an increased level of customer service. Also, evidence shows that frequent guest programmes are ineffective overall, and its use is predicted to diminish in the future. Finally, hotels must improve methods to increase customer service and satisfaction
Theme 5: **travel and tourism management**	Incentive travel marketing; special interest travel market; sustaining tourism; environmental programmes in hotels; recovery marketing and disaster planning; economic impact of tourism	Tourism development is an important vehicle in improving a country's economy and social status. Thus, to maintain sustainable tourism, developers need to co-operate with government authorities and local hospitality industries to establish environmental programmes and disaster planning methods

communication is needed among educators and industry professionals in the hospitality industry. Hospitality education must also refocus its energy on serving the needs of the hospitality industry, while considering the global community as well. The industry needs to provide more quality training programmes, which may involve taking advantage of interactive training methods to go along with supervised training.

Sridhar Prabhu
*Challenges for hospitality and
tourism operators: a North
American perspective*

- There is a need for organizations to increase employee motivation through involvement. Empowerment is cited as a key to increasing employee motivation, reducing turnover, and improving productivity. To handle employee turnover and burnout, management also needs to focus on providing a supportive organizational environment. Finally, management must be cognizant on dealing with legal matters pertaining to employment, including the employee disability and sexual harassment rulings.
- Technological innovations are present and will continue to affect the hospitality and tourism industry. Technology not only increases operational efficiency, but contributes to an increased level of guest service. Hospitality firms must take advantage of the current and future advantages of technology.
- Customer service and satisfaction are and will continue to be key issues in the hospitality industry. Methods are being continuously used and developed by industry to measure consumers' expectations in relation to satisfaction. These methods can be used along with proper employee training and operating procedures to enhance total customer service and satisfaction.
- Marketing strategy and segmentation remains a vital part of the hospitality and tourism business. Marketing strategy seems to be evolving as consumer lifestyle and purpose of travel are becoming more important, in terms of segmentation, rather than the traditional segmentation based

age, income, or nationality. Hotels and restaurants are also experimenting with unique marketing and pricing strategies, such as psychological pricing and frequent guest programmes, to influence consumer purchasing behaviour.
- Tourism development is an important vehicle in improving a country's economy and social status. Thus, to maintain sustainable tourism, developers need to co-operate with government authorities and local hospitality industries to establish environmental programmes and disaster planning methods.

A summary of the main themes and sub-themes is presented in Table VI and Figure 1.

References
(All the following references are from *Cornell Hotel and Restaurant Administration Quarterly*)

1 Haywood, K.M., "Effective training: toward a strategic approach", Vol. 33 No. 6, 1992, pp. 43-52.
2 Conrade, G., Woods, R. and Ninemeier, J., "Training in the US lodging industry: Perception and reality", Vol. 35 No. 5, 1994, pp. 16-21.
3 Shaw, M. and Patterson, J., "Management-development programs: a Canadian perspective", Vol. 36 No. 1, 1995, pp. 34-9.
4 Goodman, R.J. and Sprague, L.G., "The future of hospitality education: meeting the industry's needs", Vol. 32 No. 2, 1991, pp. 66-9.
5 Evans, M.R., "Graduate education: the next frontier", Vol. 31 No. 2, 1990, pp. 92-4.
6 Clark, J.J. and Arbel, A., "Producing global managers: the need for a new academic paradigm", Vol. 34 No. 4, 1993, pp. 83-9.
7 Durocher, J.F. and Goodman, R.J., "Training program expectations: a conundrum", Vol. 32 No. 2, 1991, pp. 76-8.
8 Durocher, J.F., "Beating the training challenge with interactive videodiscs", Vol. 31 No. 1, 1990, pp. 39-45.
9 Harris, K.J. and West, J.J., "Using multimedia in hospitality training", Vol. 34 No. 4, 1993, pp. 75-82.
10 Sternberg, L.E., "Empowerment: trust vs. control", Vol. 33 No. 1, 1992, pp. 68-72.
11 Simons, T. and Enz, C.A., "Motivating hotel employees: beyond the carrot and the stick", Vol. 36 No. 1, 1995, pp. 20-7.
12 Hogan, J.J., "Employee turnover and what to do about it", Vol. 33 No. 1, 1992, pp. 40-5.
13 Kennedy, D.J. and Berger, F., "Newcomer socialization: oriented to facts or feelings?", Vol. 35 No. 6, 1994, pp. 47-57.
14 Murthy, B. and Murrman, S.K., "Employee leasing: an alternative staffing strategy", Vol. 34 No. 3, 1993, pp. 18-23.
15 Vallen, G.K., "Organizational climate and burnout", Vol. 34 No. 1, 1993, pp. 54-9.

Figure 1
Challenges faced by the hospitality and tourism industries

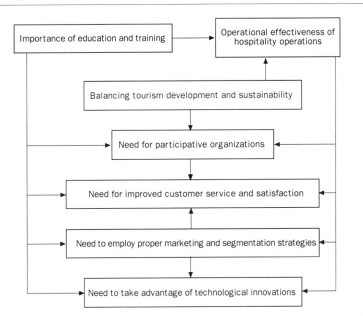

16 Tabacchi, M.H., Krone, C. and Farber, B., "A support system to mitigate manager burnout", Vol. 31 No. 3, 1990, pp. 32-7.

17 Hamilton, A.J., Aaron T. and Dry, E., "Sexual harassment: the hostile work environment and sexual harassment in the hospitality industry", Vol. 33 No. 2, 1992, pp. 88-92.

18 Sherry, J.E.H., "Employer liability for GMs' sexual harassment – a recurring workplace problem", Vol. 36 No. 4, 1995, pp. 16-17.

19 Woods, R.H. and Kavanaugh, R.R., "Here comes the ADA are you ready? (Part 1)", Vol. 33 No. 1, 1992, pp. 24-32.

20 Pellissier, J.L., "Avoiding the wrongful termination pitfall", Vol. 31 No. 1, 1990, pp. 118-23.

21 Panyko, F., "Challenging directions in food marketing", Vol. 31 No. 1, 1990, pp. 52-55.

22 Muller, C.C. and Woods, R.H., "An expanded restaurant typology", Vol. 35 No. 3, 1994, pp. 27-37.

23 Carmin, J. and Norkus, G.X., "Pricing strategies for restaurants: magic or myth?," Vol. 31 No. 3, 1990, pp. 44-50.

24 Goldman, J.B. and Eyster, J.J., "Hotel F&B leases: the view from the restaurant", Vol. 33 No. 5, 1992, pp. 72-83.

25 Paul, R.N., "Status and outlook of the chain-restaurant industry", Vol. 35 No. 3, 1994, pp. 23-6.

26 Shriber, M., Muller, C. and Inman, C., "Population changes and restaurant success", Vol. 36 No. 3, 1995, pp. 43-9.

27 Muller, C.C. and Inman, C., "The geodemographics of restaurant development", Vol. 35 No. 3, 1994, pp. 88-95.

28 Dube, L., Renaghan, L.M. and Miller, J.M., "Measuring customer satisfaction for strategic management", Vol. 35 No. 1, 1994, pp. 39-47.

29 Stevens, P., Knutson, B. and Patton, M., "DINESERV: a tool for measuring service quality in restaurants", Vol. 36 No. 2, 1995, pp. 56-60.

30 Kasanava, M.L, "Computers and multiunit food-service operations", Vol. 35 No. 3, 1994, pp. 72-80.

31 Kasanava, M.L., "PC-based registers: the next generation of point-of-sale technology", Vol. 36 No. 2, 1995, pp. 50-5.

32 Mehta, S.C. and Vera, A., "Segmentation in Singapore", Vol. 31 No. 1, 1990, pp. 80-7.

33 Hanks, R.D., Cross, R.G. and Noland, R.P., "Discounting in the hotel industry: a new approach", Vol. 33 No. 1, 1992, pp. 15-23.

34 Toh, R.S, Hu, M.Y. and Withiam, G., "Service: the key to frequent guest programs", Vol. 34 No. 3, 1993, pp. 66-71.

35 McCleary, K.W. and Weaver, P.A., "Are frequent guest programs effective?," Vol. 32 No. 2, 1991, pp. 38-45.

36 Lewis, R.C. and Nightingale, M., "Targeting service to your customer", Vol. 32 No. 2, 1991, pp. 18-27.

37 Barsky, J. and Labagh, C.C., "Theory S: total customer service", Vol. 31 No. 1, 1990, pp. 88-95.

38 Emmer, R.M., Tauck, C. and Wilkinson, S., "Marketing hotels using global distribution systems", Vol. 34 No. 6, 1993, pp. 80-9.

39 Reid, R.D. and Sandler, M., "The use of technology to improve service quality", Vol. 33 No. 3, 1992, pp. 68-73.

40 Warren, P. and Ostergren, N.W., "Marketing your hotel: challenges of the '90s", Vol. 31 No. 1, 1990, pp. 56-9.

41 Mehta, S.C., Loh, J.C.M. and Mehta, S.S., "Incentive-travel marketing: the Singapore approach", Vol. 32 No. 3, 1991, pp. 67-74.

42 Sorensen, L., "The special-interest travel market", Vol. 34 No. 3, 1993, pp. 24-30.

43 Durocher, J., "Recovery marketing: what to do after a natural disaster", Vol. 35 No. 2, 1994, pp. 66-71.

44 Drabek, T.E., "Disaster planning and response by tourist business executives", Vol. 36 No. 3, 1995, pp. 86-96.

45 Manning, E.W. and Dougherty, T.D., "Sustaining tourism: preserving the golden goose", Vol. 36 No. 2, 1995, pp. 29-42.

46 Iwanowski, K. and Rushmore, C., "Introducing the eco-friendly hotel", Vol. 35 No. 1, 1994, pp. 34-8.

47 Khan, H., Phang, S. and Toh, R.S., "Singapore's hospitality industry: the multiplier effect", Vol. 36 No. 1, 1995, pp. 64-9.

Hospitality operations: patterns in management, service improvement and business performance

Richard Teare

Research Director (Europe) Worldwide Hospitality and Tourism Trends,
University of Surrey, Guildford, UK

Provides an overview of
developments in hospitality
operations management as
reflected by articles published in: *International Journal of Contemporary Hospitality Management, Interna-
tional Journal of Hospitality
Management, International
Journal of Service Industry
Management* and *Service
Industries Journal* during
1995 (business performance,
customers and service
improvement, operations and
the curriculum, strategy and
development) and during the
six-year period 1989-1994
(structural relationships in
hospitality and tourism,
operations and business
development, strategy and
systems development, human
resource development and
quality improvements).

Introduction

The aim of this article is to review emerging themes and sub-themes as reflected by articles published during 1995 in the *International Journal of Contemporary Hospitality Management, International Journal of Hospitality Management, International Journal of Service Industry Management* and the *Service Industries Journal*. The second part of the article reflects on patterns of thinking and development by drawing on literature from the same journals published over a six-year period (1989-1994). A summary of the issues raised in the article is provided in the form of two thematic diagrams relating to 1995 and 1989-1994 respectively.

A review of 1995

The commentary is derived from a thematic framework encompassing four themes:
1 business performance;
2 customers and service improvement;
3 operations and the curriculum;
4 strategy and development.

Theme 1: business performance

The notion of "excellence" introduced by Peters and Waterman in the early 1980s was derived from a study of successful firms, some of whom were unable to sustain their achievements in the longer term. Caruana *et al.*[1] evaluate the concept of business excellence using a modelling technique known as EXCEL and a sample of large UK service firms. While organizations strive for excellence, individual managers are often left to unravel the puzzle for themselves and Peacock[2] analyses the tensions between different notions of "success" as they relate to the institutional settings in which hospitality managers work. He concludes that there is no one "correct" definition of good job performance as the working environment, the type of operation and the type of manager influence how the job components are defined and the criteria for successfully achieving them.

Managers depend on an array of tools to gauge workplace success and it can be argued that a balanced set of measurements are needed. Brander Brown and McDonnell[3] investigate whether the balanced score-card performance measurement method provides a practical solution. They found that hotel general managers saw benefits in preparing a detailed score-card for each of the areas or departments controlled by senior managers within an individual hotel, providing the score-cards are reviewed and updated regularly. In this way, unit management teams can share the responsibility for achieving goals relating to a set of critical success factors for the unit as a whole. Yasin and Zimmerer[4] link the application of benchmarking to the hotel's ability to achieve its goals in the area of quality improvement. They present a practical framework for this which defines both the operating and service subsystems of the hotel and propose specific methods for quality improvement in each.

Information technology provides a feasible way of harnessing full operational capability and Donaghy *et al.*[5] review the application of yield management to profit maximization. A common use is to compute market sensitive pricing of fixed hotel room capacity for specific market segments. The authors examine this and provide a structured operational framework for focusing on ten key areas in hospitality operations. The main challenge is to engage the full potential of information technology and Crichton and Edgar[6] argue that the key element in managing complexity is to seek a balance between supply and demand-side technology. They foresee that as technology develops further, the concept of managing complexity as opposed to simply minimizing or adapting to it will become more important (see Table I).

Theme 2: customers and service improvement

The concept of mass customization has emerged in part, from a decade of debate centred on the mass production of inexpensive, commodity-like products or services (the assembly line approach) on the one hand and premium-priced, individually-tailored and highly differentiated offerings on the

Richard Teare
*Hospitality operations:
patterns in management,
service improvement and
business performance*

Table I
Business performance

Authors	Focus	Sub-theme
Caruana et al.[1]	Evaluates the concept of business excellence using a modelling technique known as EXCEL and a sample of large UK service firms	Business excellence
Peacock[2]	Analyses the tensions between different notions of "success" as they relate to the institutional settings in which hospitality managers work	Job performance
Brander Brown and McDonnell[3]	Investigates whether the balanced score-card performance measurement method provides a sufficiently quick yet comprehensive view of unit performance	Performance measurement
Yasin and Zimmorer[4]	Links the application of benchmarking to the hotel's ability to achieve continuous quality improvement Defines both the operating and service subsystems of the hotel and proposes specific methods for quality improvement in each	Benchmarking and quality improvement
Donaghy et al.[5]	Reviews yield management – a profit maximization strategy – in relation to the market sensitive pricing of fixed hotel room capacity relative to specific market segments.	Yield management and profit performance
Crichton and Edgar[6]	Argues that as technology develops further, the concept of managing complexity as opposed to simply minimizing or adapting to it will become more widespread	Information technology and competitiveness

other. Hart[7] observes that much of the power of mass customization, like total quality management before it, lies in its visionary and strategic implications. Its application should enable companies to produce affordable, high-quality goods and services, but with shorter cycle times and lower costs. The key dimensions of his diagnostic framework for assessing the potential for mass customization are: customer sensitivity, process amenability, competitive environment and organizational readiness. Taylor and Lyon[8] discuss the application of mass customization to food service operations and its likely adoption in a rapidly maturing marketplace. A compatible step is for management to create an appropriate form of internal customer orientation and Stauss[9] notes that a deliberate and sustained effort is needed to create a climate that promotes a customer's viewpoint of work activities, processes and non-standardized support services. Customer orientation also implies a readiness to measure, and where necessary improve, the quality of service and support in keeping with customer expectations. Lee and Hing[10] assess the usefulness and application of the SERVQUAL technique in measuring service quality in the fine dining sector. They demonstrate how easily and inexpensively the technique can be used to identify the strengths and weaknesses of individual restaurants' service dimensions. A periodic audit of customer service deliverables might also be usefully conducted and Congram and Epelman[11] recommend the use of the structured analysis and design technique (SADT). This enables service providers to review the processes in which they participate, identify, implement and review improvements in service delivery and rethink aspects of the service package.

The interpersonal aspects of service delivery are potentially the most difficult to audit and improve. A useful starting point is to undertake a programme of job analysis for service staff to identify the best fit between tasks, behaviours and personal attributes. Papadopoulou et al.[12] identify the dimensions of a higher customer contact food and beverage operative's job as perceived by managers, supervisors and operatives and examine within-source and between source-differences in perceptions. Their study confirms the versatility of job analysis as an organizational and diagnostic tool. Among other uses, it depicts the dimensions of a job, the related personal qualities and experience and the training implications. In most cases, it is also helpful to profile ideal combinations of age and experience for different service roles, especially as the industry relies heavily on younger workers[13].

Corporate level concern about service quality issues has stimulated interest in employee empowerment. In theory, empowered

Richard Teare
*Hospitality operations:
patterns in management,
service improvement and
business performance*

employees will be more committed to ensuring that service encounters satisfy customers as they have the necessary discretion and autonomy to "delight the customer". Lashley[14] explores the implications of empowering employees and provides a framework for understanding managerial motives in selecting different forms of empowerment and their consequences for achieving improvements in customer service quality. To support empowerment and other customer-led initiatives, training and development is needed. Clements and Josiam[15] outline a step-by-step procedure to evaluate both the costs and the benefits of any training proposal. Their approach utilizes a financial analysis model for identifying the dollar value of both performance outcomes and training costs. While interpersonal skills development and support is needed for service staff, supervisors and

managers need to make appropriate decisions and Gore[16] examines some of the theoretical models of decision making derived from the field of psychology and considers the related implications for training in decision making (see Table II).

Theme 3: operations and the curriculum

While industry and education necessarily contextualize their own agendas for learning and development, they might be expected to converge around the core skills and knowledge that operatives, supervisors and managers need in order to function effectively in the workplace. Nebel *et al.*[17] traced the career paths of hotel general managers (GMs) in American mid-range, upscale and luxury

Table II
Customers and service improvement

Authors	Focus	Sub-theme
Hart[7]	Proposes that much of the power of mass customization, like total quality management before it, lies in its visionary and strategic implications	Concepts of mass customization
Taylor and Lyon[8]	Argues that "mass customization" is replacing standardization in food service operations	Customization and fast food
Stauss[9]	Argues that internal customer orientation does not occur naturally but from management decisions which bring about an appropriate setting	Customer orientation
Lee and Hing[10]	Assesses the usefulness and application of the SERVQUAL instrument in measuring and comparing service quality in the fine dining sector	Measuring service quality
Congram and Epelman[11]	Recommends the use of the structured analysis and design technique (SADT) to review service processes, achieve improvements in service delivery and design a service	Process evaluation and improvement
Papadopoulou *et al.*[12]	Identifies the dimensions of a higher customer contact food and beverage operative's job as perceived by managers, supervisors and operatives and examines differences in perceptions	Service performance
Lucas[13]	Reports a study of age-related issues in hotel and catering employment and confirms high reliance on younger workers	Age and industry employment
Lashley[14]	Provides a framework for understanding managerial motives in selecting different forms of empowerment – a concept that is largely concerned with the improvement of customer service quality	Empowerment and customer service improvement
Clements and Josiam[15]	Outlines a step-by-step procedure to evaluate both the costs and the benefits of any training proposal. The approach utilizes a financial analysis model to identify the dollar value of training inputs	Training and performance-related outcomes
Gore[16]	Examines some of the theoretical models of human decision making derived from the field of psychology and considers some of the important issues this raises for training in decision making	Training and decision making

Richard Teare
*Hospitality operations:
patterns in management,
service improvement and
business performance*

hotels and found that the two main operational departments, food and beverage (F & B) and rooms, account for three-quarters of the GM career paths, with F & B representing 45 per cent. This relatively narrow focus reflects a traditional emphasis on gaining practical experience in operations management and other studies such as the one conducted by Hsu and Gregory[18], have sought to identify an industry professional's view of the competences needed for entry-level hotel management.

In "New visions for hospitality operations management" (*IJCHM*, Vol. 7 No. 5) Johns and Teare[19] outline some of the changes that have occurred in the hospitality business environment during the 1990s and review changes in skills, attitudes and competences the industry now requires. It is evident that a more robust systems approach is needed in response to a dynamically changing industry and Jones and Lockwood[20] provide a conceptual framework for reconciling traditional thinking about the hospitality operations management curriculum with a multi-level view of operating systems, process and output analysis. Kirk[21] reviews the systems approach to problem solving and operational management, including the differentiation between hard and soft systems. He argues that given the occurrence in most problem situations of both technical and human dimensions, a hybrid of scientific, hard systems and soft systems methodologies will give the best solution. In making systems work, Edwards and Ingram[22] contend that many of the techniques more usually associated with manufacturing industries such as capacity, forecasting, managing demand and scheduling can be just as easily applied to hospitality operations. Harris[23] goes further and demonstrates the application of accounting techniques to management decision making in operational settings and explains how closer integration might be achieved in the hospitality operations curriculum. In sum, these contributions contend that a broader-based view of operating systems is needed and that a more holistic approach to operations management is desirable in responding to the challenges and opportunities brought about by a rapid pace of change. If new thinking is reflected in the curriculum, then to some extent students on placement (and later as new entrants) will stimulate dialogue between industry and education provided that the "old" problems faced by experienced managers are addressed too. Ford and LeBruto[24] illustrate how aspects of curriculum innovation might be evaluated in their study of perceptions of experiential learning requirements of students

and new entrants while Yu and Huat[25] use a perception study to examine and analyse cultural differences in managing hotel operations among experienced, expatriate professionals (see Table III).

Theme 4: Strategy and development

The interplay between market conditions and the characteristic properties of any given market segment is difficult to assess unless an observable change is occurring. Nield and Peacock[26] report on a transition in the UK brewing industry brought about by a greater degree of concentration during the past five years, mainly owin to regulatory intervention. They observe that if further intervention is imposed at a European level, the UK brewing business is likely to be characterized by single focus strategies and become a more brand oriented, market-led industry at the expense of competition and ultimately of the consumer. The fastest-growing sector of the hospitality industry in the USA is gaming-related business and Atkinson and LeBruto[27] report on a study of the expectations of the investment community that is underpinning its expansion. Specifically, they sought to determine whether investors acquiring stock at the initial offering price earn large returns on their investment, and their findings support this hypothesis.

Industry strategy is widely reported in the literature and there are several notable sub-themes. Becker and Olsen[28] assess the appropriateness of generic management approaches to managing hospitality organizations and conclude that an over-reliance on generic strategy is likely to have a detrimental effect on the distinctiveness that hospitality firms seek to create in competing for market share. Collier and Gregory[29] explore the expanding role of strategic management accounting (SMA) in the hotel sector through case studies derived from six UK hotel groups.

SMA is defined as: "the provision and analysis of management accounting data relating to business strategy: particularly the relative levels and trends in real costs and prices, volumes, market share, cash flow and the demands on a firm's total resources". Their study shows that the accounting function in hotel groups is becoming increasingly involved in strategic management accounting, both in planning and in *ad hoc* exercises on the market conditions and competitor analysis. The issue of internationalization is addressed by Burgess *et al.*[30], who present a critical evaluation of the literature relating to

Richard Teare
*Hospitality operations:
patterns in management,
service improvement and
business performance*

Table III
Operations and the curriculum

Authors	Focus	Sub-theme
Nebel *et al.*[17]	Reports on a study of the career paths of hotel general managers in American mid-range, up-scale and luxury hotels	Hotel general manager career paths
Hsu and Gregory[18]	Investigates and identifies the competences needed for entry-level hotel managers from the industry professional's point of view	Entry-point competences for hotel managers
Johns and Teare[19]	Outlines the changes that have occurred in the hospitality business environment and reviews the changes in skills, attitudes and competences the industry now requires	Re-aligning the curriculum
Jones and Lockwood[20]	Reconciles the traditional view of hospitality operations based on process analysis, by identifying four levels of hospitality operations management	Operations and systems design
Kirk[21]	Reviews the development of a systems approach to problem solving and operational management, including the differentiation between hard and soft systems	The curriculum and system theory
Edwards and Ingram[22]	Argues that many of the techniques in operations management normally associated with manufacturing industries can be just as easily applied to the hospitality industry	Manufacturing principles and service operations
Harris[23]	Presents an approach to hospitality operations curriculum development which relates to the hospitality product and the management decision making involved in operations management	Managerial decision making
Ford and LeBruto[24]	Investigates the optimum time that hotel management students should spend in an experiential learning or "hands on" environment	Experiential learning and the curriculum
Yu and Huat[25]	Examines and analyses the perceptions of six management difficulty factors by expatriate hotel professionals working in China	Competences for expatriate managers

the internationalization of hotel groups, previous "success studies" and prescriptive strategic management models in relation to multinational hotel groups. Finally, the relationship between strategy formulation and decision making is examined by Ogden[31] who uses in-depth case studies to study the process of strategic decision making arising from the management of compulsory competitive tendering for catering and cleaning services, following the 1988 Local Government Act.

The role of employees in organizations, especially in relation to development issues, is reflected in a number of areas. Royle[32] examines the human resource policy of the McDonald's Corporation via its operations in Germany and the UK. The study focuses on the makeup of the workforce, levels of unionization and worker participation. These issues are analysed in the context of the debate about the convergence or divergence of behaviour in organizations and the increasing globalization or economic activity. Moutinho *et al.*[33] describe the findings of a

positivistic comparative study undertaken in three different European countries to assess the perceptions of British, Irish and Spanish hotel managers. The study sought to relate managers' opinions on a number of key issues to the future development of the hotel sector. All the participating managers expressed concerns about the conservation of cultural heritage, the protection of buildings and the local countryside, as well as the need for the global protection of the environment. This issue is explored in some detail by Ayala[34] who reviews strategies adopted by the international hotel industry for achieving greater environmental sensitivity and sustainability (see Table IV).

A review of emerging patterns: 1989 to 1994

Structural relationships in hospitality and tourism
Tourism is an attractive and important industry for many small and developing nations. In

Richard Teare
*Hospitality operations:
patterns in management,
service improvement and
business performance*

Table IV
Strategy and development

Authors	Focus	Sub-theme
Nield and Peacock[26]	Because of regulatory intervention, the UK brewing industry has become increasingly concentrated. Asserts that if further intervention is imposed at a European level, the trend will continue	Industry structure and Government policy
Atkinson and LeBruto[27]	The fastest growing segment of the hospitality industry is gaming-related business. Reports on a study to determine whether investors acquiring stock at the initial offering price earn large returns	Growth sectors and the investment community
Becker and Olsen[28]	Explores the role of heterogeneity in the study of service organizations and illustrates the ill effects that can result when generic strategies are applied indiscriminately	Sector specific or generic strategy?
Collier and Gregory[29]	Explores the use which is made of strategic management accounting in the hotel sector through case studies at six major UK hotel groups	Strategic management accounting
Burgess *et al.*[30]	Reviews the literature relating to the internationalization of hotel groups, prior "success studies" and prescriptive trategic management models in relation to multinational hotel groups	Internationalization and successful growth
Ogden[31]	Examines the process of strategic decision making arising from the management of compulsory competitive tendering (CCT) for catering and cleaning services following the 1988 Local Government Act	Strategy, structure and employee relations
Royle[32]	Examines the human resource policy of the McDonald's Corporation via its operations in Germany and the UK. Focuses on the makeup of the workforce, levels of unionization and worker participation	Internationalization and industrial relations strategy
Moutinho *et al.*[33]	Describes the findings of a positivistic comparative study undertaken in three different European countries to assess the perceptions of British, Irish and Spanish hotel managers	Perspectives on hotel sector development
Ayala[34]	Assesses hotel sector strategies for achieving greater environmental sensitivity and sustainability from three perspectives: ecotechniques, environmental sponsorship and econ-packaging	Environmentally sensitive design

Singapore, for example, tourism has been found to promote cultural diversity, a sense of cleanliness and a feeling of pride[35]. Countries new to tourism, however, need to consider the primary needs of foreign visitors. In a study by Olokesusi[36] in Abeokuta, Nigeria, tourists are encouraged to visit the densely populated town that is suffering from noise pollution, lack of telephones, unreliable water and electricity supplies. Countries with developed tourist industries such as Bali[37] and parts of Mexico[38] face widely differing challenges though, in essence, matching supply and demand and protecting tourism receipts from inflation are key priorities. Europe cannot afford to be complacent about traditional tourism markets. Although European tourism policies provide co-ordination and support on planning and other matters, member states need to develop their own strategies if they wish to maximize incoming tourism. This is partly because fellow EC members compete with each other for tourism revenue[39].

Commercial success depends on careful marketing planning so as to offer the international tourist an array of benefits and facilities which compare favourably with competing tourism destinations. The prerequisites for attracting foreign visitors are: a transportation infrastructure; hotel and restaurant facilities and a safe and secure environment.

Operations and business development

While internal systems and procedures are important mechanisms, Kim and Olsen[40] advocate a balanced approach by monitoring events occurring in the external domain and assessing the potential impact on business

Richard Teare
*Hospitality operations:
patterns in management,
service improvement and
business performance*

and unit level operations. External awareness is also influencing trends in facilities management and design. Improvements in energy conservation and recycling mean that "green" marketing strategies will be more widely adopted in the future, especially as new design technologies enable hotels and resorts to use natural resources more efficiently[41]. The notion of an "intelligent bedroom" which uses new generation information technologies for global communications and to monitor and adjust energy usage, especially when the room is not in use, will help to establish a new design standard for construction. Coupled with this, productivity and performance improvements could be readily made by wider adoption of yield management systems.

A growing body of evidence suggests that service firms are experimenting with a wide array of approaches and methods designed to narrow the gap between the provider and the consumer of services. Edvardsson[42] argues that it is not sufficient to focus on the encounter with the customer but that organizations should study all the critical incidents in the production chain so as to derive a deeper understanding of how weaknesses affect customer satisfaction with the end product.

The alignment between groups of customers which constitute market segments, product specification and consistent service delivery reflects the product differentiation challenge. It seems likely that brands based on customized service packages will be needed in the future so that marketing strategy emphasizes service enhancement as well as socially and ecological responsible leisure and tourism experiences.

Strategy and systems development
The literature reveals that some interesting strategic planning adaptations are currently being tested. Among these, Armistead[43] has elaborated a framework for a service operations strategy that emphasizes consistent service delivery in keeping with the expectations of customers. Contributions in other areas include innovative approaches to strategic marketing planning and the use of computer modelling and simulation in locational analysis and market segmentation. Overall, the broad-ranging nature of published work points to a lack of systematic planning, especially in relation to external analysis and the application of decision-making models and techniques to planning tasks and activities. Evidence suggests that more collaborative research is needed in these areas with the objective of enabling

hospitality firms to systemize their planning effort and release more time for creative thinking and innovation. Yet, there are some indications that systematic financial analysis produces a number of positive outcomes, especially in terms of organizational performance. While computer technology can assist financial analysis and decision making, a consensus of opinion exists both in industry and education that hospitality managers need to be able to interpret financial data in order to derive benefits from investing in financial information systems. In response, Harris[44] proposes an approach to financial planning using computer-based spreadsheets. The spreadsheet models need not be large or complex to assist management decision making in an array of financial planning and control situations.

The pace of change in the external business environment means that systematic external analysis is an essential precursor to decision making and strategy formulation. Evidence shows that the principles of environmental scanning have not been widely adopted and that hospitality business executives are in fact increasingly concerned about sources of uncertainty and ways of assessing possible impacts more accurately in the future. Coupled with this, the strategic role of information systems has yet to be fully appreciated.

Human resource development
In general terms, rates of innovation in hospitality and tourism have been held back by traditional methods and practices. This is particularly the case in the human resources field where low pay, low esteem jobs have contributed to high rates of labour turnover. There are however, signs that different approaches to managing and deploying human resources are being tried. Several writers have reported encouraging results from studies of flexible working, and Luckock concludes that job roles can be re-shaped in a more flexible way to suit both employees and employers[45,46]. A more imaginative approach is needed, though, as a good deal more could be done to make jobs more interesting, less stressful and less unsocial from the employee's viewpoint. In the managerial domain, while many experienced hospitality managers have enjoyed successful careers and seem well suited to the nature of the work involved, there are some indications that managerial roles are becoming more stressful. There are a number of key contributory factors and these include the breadth of choice available to consumers in mature markets, the pressure to "do more with fewer people" to preserve or enhance profit margins

Richard Teare
*Hospitality operations:
patterns in management,
service improvement and
business performance*

and the pace of change in business and commerce as a whole. In response, some organizations are seeking to build on the skills, talents and experience available to them by establishing a "learning organization" culture, climate and approach to business and human resource development.

Evidence suggests that hospitality firms are generally bound by traditional working methods and employment policy in comparison with other service firms. A more open-minded approach is needed to maximize the potential that exists in the industry's skilled and unskilled workforce. The concept of lifelong learning and the mechanisms for supporting this in hospitality organizations are yet to be firmly established. The impact of new technology, maturing markets, recession and other agents of change means that managers, supervisors and operatives need to adapt and regularly update their skills and knowledge base. This calls for a closer partnership between industry and education and more flexible, work-based delivery mechanisms for education and training.

Quality improvement

Quality management encompasses a broad range of activity – from organization-wide total quality efforts to perceptions of service quality by customers experiencing service. Silvestro *et al.*[47] observe that many service companies are developing their own systems for monitoring and measuring aspects of service quality. These include measures for internal, external, "hard" and "soft" performance indicators and for tangible and intangible aspects of service. In hospitality and tourism services, it is an observable fact that a similar range of topics are being covered, especially in relation to: the role of quality in establishing competitive advantage and securing market share; the cost of quality (and of non-conformance); the measurement of quality and systems for assuring quality.

If service standards are to improve, service personnel need to be open to new and innovative ways of improving service delivery. The key implication here is that managers should seek to create an organizational atmosphere which supports efforts to improve quality and enhances the nature of communications between employees and customers[48]. In part, the personalities of service staff determine the extent to which employees are well suited to the role they perform. In this context, employee selection methods that draw on biodata profiling and personality assessment have been shown to work effectively[49]. The diffusion and adoption of these and similar selection techniques may assist

efforts to reduce labour turnover and improve customer satisfaction levels by defining the job-person fit for different job roles.

The means by which excellent service is guaranteed to customers is a topical issue and there appears to be much scope for further research and innovation. The methods used by industry to track customer satisfaction are typically incomplete or inadequate with few exceptions, and more work is needed, especially in relating customer expectations of service performance. Further, organizational efforts to guarantee service excellence requires a supportive infrastructure that equips and empowers staff to respond to all customers in the supply chain, not just the external customer at the end of the line. The concept of continuous quality improvement (CQI) has yet to make a significant impact on the international hospitality business, yet it appears inevitable if organizations wish to establish a quality-driven culture. Cultural change will also mean a shift in traditional styles of management as team-working structures become better established with the ultimate goal of a transition to self-managed work teams.

Summary observations

The review of 1995 identifies some of the principal contributions to development and debate in four areas (see also thematic diagram in Figure 1):
- Business performance issues are explored in relation to: notions of business excellence; job performance and performance measurement; benchmarking and quality improvement; yield management and profit performance; information technology and competitiveness.
- Customers and service improvement issues address: concepts of mass customization; customer orientation; service quality measurement; process evaluation and improvement; service performance, empowerment and training.
- Operations and the curriculum reviews: career paths and competences; operations and systems design; managerial decision making and notions of experiential learning and the curriculum.
- Strategy and development considers: industry structure and development variables; strategic accounting; internationalization and environmental sensitivity.

The review of 1989-1994 reflects broader-based patterns (see thematic diagram in Figure 2) as follows:

Richard Teare
*Hospitality operations:
patterns in management,
service improvement and
business performance*

Figure 1
Review of 1995: summary of main themes and subthemes

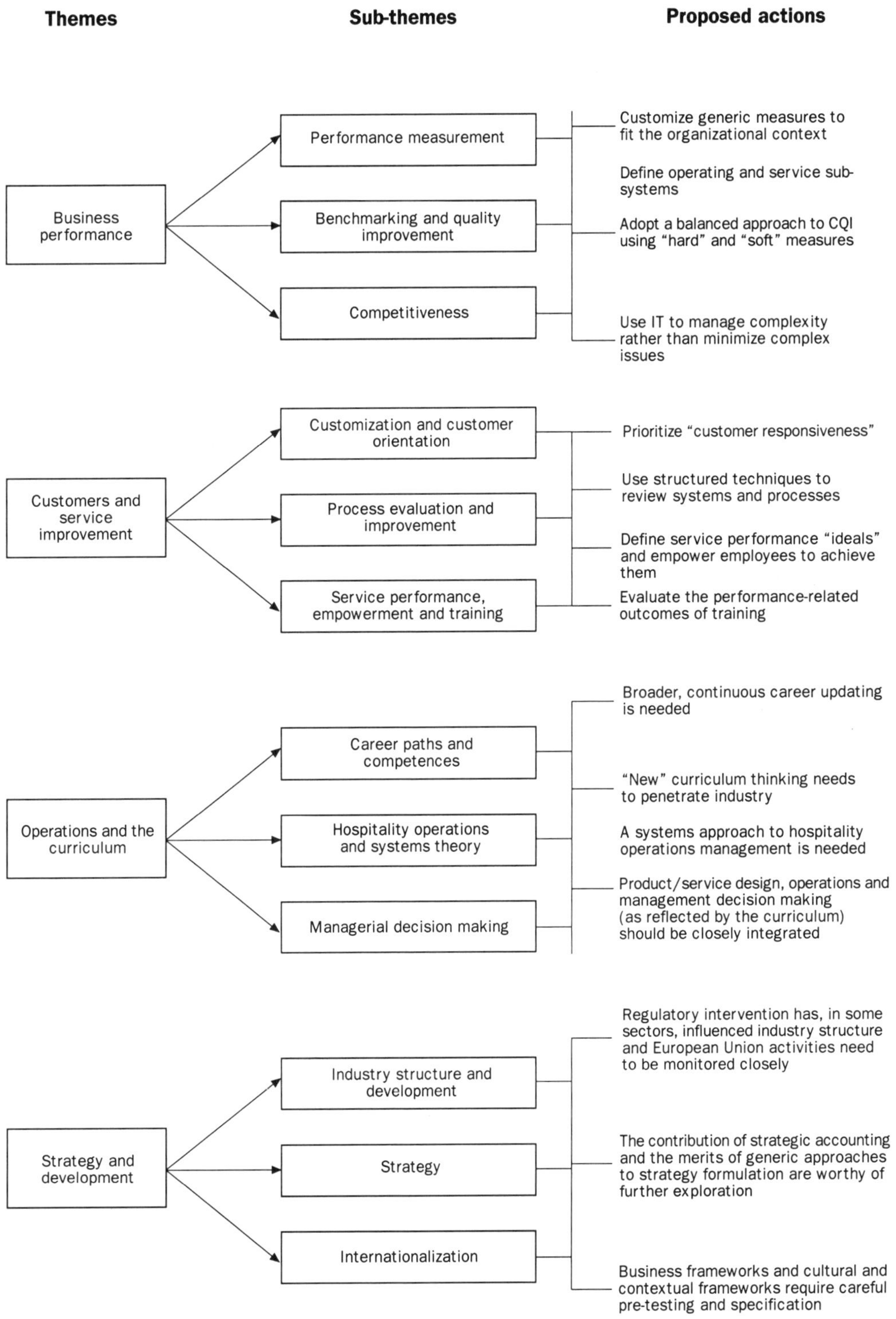

Themes	Sub-themes	Proposed actions
Business performance	Performance measurement	Customize generic measures to fit the organizational context
	Benchmarking and quality improvement	Define operating and service sub-systems Adopt a balanced approach to CQI using "hard" and "soft" measures
	Competitiveness	Use IT to manage complexity rather than minimize complex issues
Customers and service improvement	Customization and customer orientation	Prioritize "customer responsiveness"
	Process evaluation and improvement	Use structured techniques to review systems and processes Define service performance "ideals" and empower employees to achieve them
	Service performance, empowerment and training	Evaluate the performance-related outcomes of training
Operations and the curriculum	Career paths and competences	Broader, continuous career updating is needed "New" curriculum thinking needs to penetrate industry
	Hospitality operations and systems theory	A systems approach to hospitality operations management is needed
	Managerial decision making	Product/service design, operations and management decision making (as reflected by the curriculum) should be closely integrated
Strategy and development	Industry structure and development	Regulatory intervention has, in some sectors, influenced industry structure and European Union activities need to be monitored closely
	Strategy	The contribution of strategic accounting and the merits of generic approaches to strategy formulation are worthy of further exploration
	Internationalization	Business frameworks and cultural and contextual frameworks require careful pre-testing and specification

- Structural relationships in hospitality and tourism (in the context of tourism development) can help to: promote cultural diversity; encourage improvements to transport and resource infrastructures; contribute to invisible exports.

- Operations and business development (together with strategy and systems development) foresees greater interest in: environmental scanning; facilities management, communications and design technologies; energy conservation and performance improvement.

Richard Teare
*Hospitality operations:
patterns in management,
service improvement and
business performance*

Figure 2
Review of 1989-1994: summary of main themes and subthemes

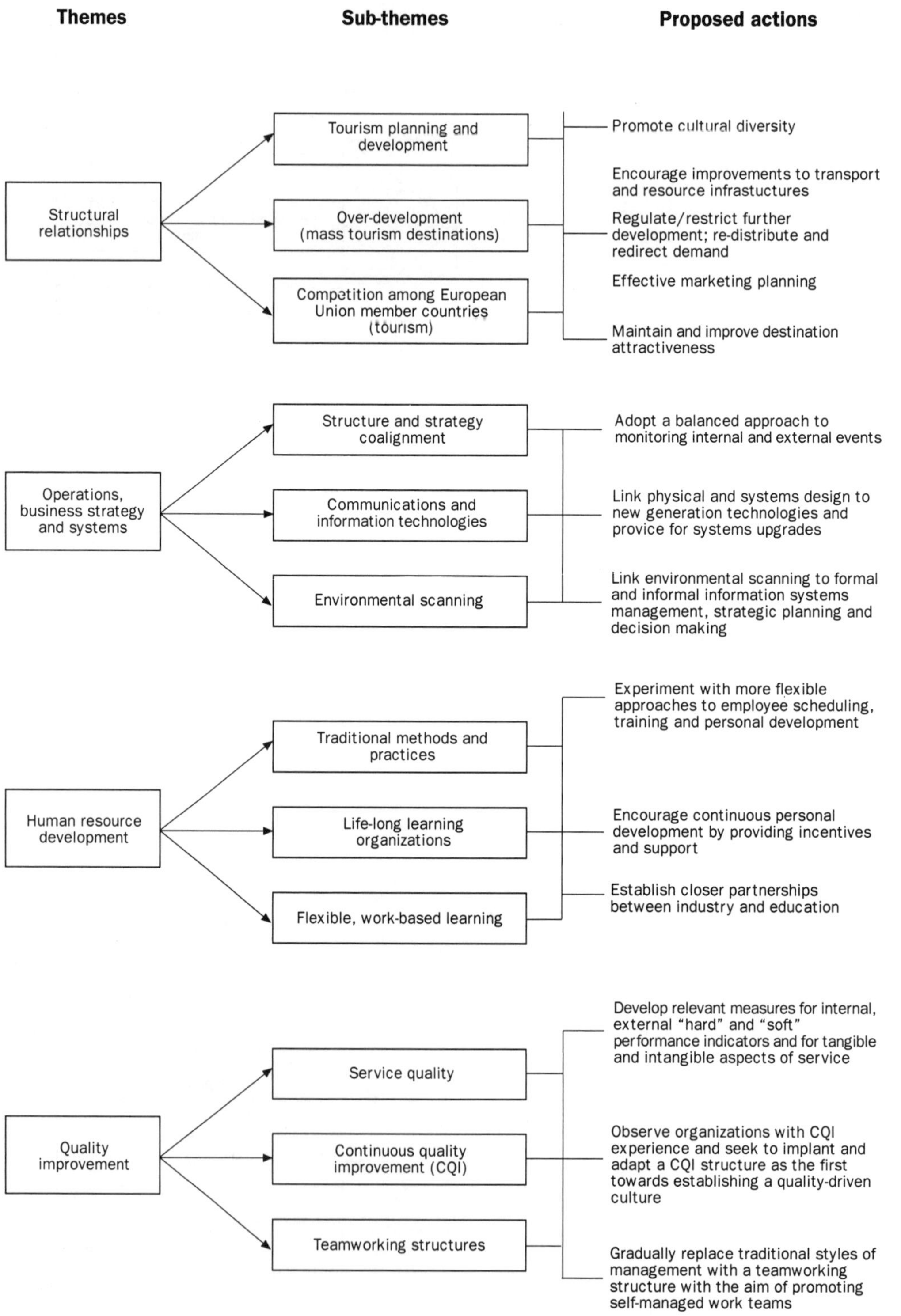

Themes	Sub-themes	Proposed actions

- Human resource development reports: a gradual evolution in working methods and employment policy characterized by a more open-minded approach; greater interest in the concept of the life-long learning organization and more flexible, work-based schemes for education and training.

- Quality improvement observes that the concept of continuous quality improvement (CQI) has not yet been widely adopted by industry, though this, a team structure and self-managed work team activity are key elements of a quality-driven organizational culture.

Richard Teare
*Hospitality operations:
patterns in management,
service improvement and
business performance*

References

1 Caruana, A., Pitt, L. F. and Morris M. H., "Are there excellent service firms, and do they perform well?", *The Service Industries Journal,* Vol. 15 No. 3, 1995, pp. 243-56.

2 Peacock, M., "A job well done: hospitality managers and success", *International Journal of Contemporary Hospitality Management,* Vol. 7 No. 2/3, 1995, pp. 48-51.

3 Brander Brown, J. and McDonnell, B., "The balanced score-card: short-term guest or long-term resident?", *International Journal of Contemporary Hospitality Management,* Vol. 7 No. 2/3, 1995, pp. 7-11.

4 Yasin, M. M. and Zimmerer, T. W. "The role of benchmarking in achieving continuous service quality", *International Journal of Contemporary Hospitality Management,* Vol. 7 No. 4, 1995, pp. 27-32.

5 Donaghy, K., McMahon, U. and McDowell, D., "Yield management: an overview", *International Journal of Hospitality Management,* Vol. 14 No. 2, 1995, pp. 139-50.

6 Crichton, E. and Edgar, D. "Managing complexity for competitive advantage: an IT perspective", *International Journal of Contemporary Hospitality Management,* Vol. 7 No. 2/3, 1995, pp. 12-18.

7 Hart, C. W. L., "Mass customization: conceptual underpinnings, opportunities and limits", *International Journal of Service Industry Management,* Vol. 6 No. 2, 1995, pp. 36-45.

8 Taylor, S. and Lyon. P., "Paradigm lost: the rise and fall of McDonaldization", *International Journal of Contemporary Hospitality Management,* Vol. 7 No. 2/3, 1995, pp. 64-8.

9 Stauss, B., "Internal services: classification and quality management", *International Journal of Service Industry Management,* Vol. 6 No. 2, 1995, pp. 62-78.

10 Lee, Y. L. and Hing, N., "Measuring quality in restaurant operations: an application of the SERVQUAL instrument", *International Journal of Hospitality Management,* Vol. 14 No. 3/4, 1995, pp. 293-310.

11 Congram, C. and Epelman, M., "How to describe your service: an invitation to the structured analysis and design technique", *International Journal of Service Industry Management,* Vol. 6 No. 2, 1995, pp. 6-23.

12 Papadopoulou, A., Ineson, E. M. and Wilkie, D. T., "Convergence between sources of service job analysis data", *International Journal of Contemporary Hospitality Management,* Vol. 7 No. 2/3, 1995, pp. 42-7.

13 Lucas, R., "Some age-related issues in hotel and catering employment", *The Service Industries Journal,* Vol. 15 No. 2, 1995, pp. 234-50.

14 Lashley, C., "Towards an understanding of employee empowerment in hospitality services", *International Journal of Contemporary Hospitality Management,* Vol. 7 No. 1, 1995, pp. 27-32.

15 Clements, C. J. and Josiam, B. M., "Training: quantifying the financial benefits", *International Journal of Contemporary Hospitality Management,* Vol. 7 No. 1, 1995, pp. 10-15.

16 Gore, J., "Hotel managers' decision making: can psychology help?", *International Journal of Contemporary Hospitality Management,* Vol. 7 No. 2/3, 1995, pp. 19-23.

17 Nebel, E. C., Lee, J-S. and Vidakovic, B., "Hotel general manager career paths in the United States", *International Journal of Hospitality Management,* Vol. 14 No. 3/4, 1995, pp. 245-60.

18 Hsu, J-F. and Gregory, S. R., "Developing future managers in Taiwan: from an industry viewpoint", *International Journal of Hospitality Management,* Vol. 14 No. 3/4, 1995, pp. 261-9.

19 Johns, N. and Teare, R., "Change, opportunity and the new operations management curriculum", *International Journal of Contemporary Hospitality Management,* Vol. 7 No. 5, 1995, pp. 4-8.

20 Jones, P. and Lockwood, A., "Hospitality operating systems", *International Journal of Contemporary Hospitality Management,* Vol. 7 No. 5, 1995, pp. 17-20.

21 Kirk, D., "Hard and soft systems: a common paradigm for operations management?", *International Journal of Contemporary Hospitality Management,* Vol. 7 No. 5, 1995, pp. 13-16.

22 Edwards, J. S. A. and Ingram, H., "Food, beverage and accommodation: an integrated operations approach", *International Journal of Contemporary Hospitality Management,* Vol. 7 No. 5, 1995, pp. 25-8.

23 Harris, P., "A development strategy for the hospitality operations management curriculum", *International Journal of Contemporary Hospitality Management,* Vol. 7 No. 5, 1995, pp. 29-32.

24 Ford, R. C. and LeBruto, S. M., "How much practical hotel management education is necessary?", *International Journal of Contemporary Hospitality Management,* Vol. 7 No. 5, 1995, pp. i-iv.

25 Yu, L. and Huat, G. S., "Perceptions of management difficulty factors by expatriate hotel professionals in China", *International Journal of Hospitality Management,* Vol. 14 No. 3/4, 1995, pp. 375-88.

26 Nield, K. and Peacock, G., "Competition in the U. K. beer market: further intervention in the U. K. beer market may produce a brand oriented market at the expense of competition and consumer choice", *International Journal of Hospitality Management,* Vol. 14 No. 2, 1995, pp. 103-6.

27 Atkinson, S. M. and LeBruto S. M., "Initial public offerings in the gaming industry: an empirical study", *International Journal of Hospitality Management,* Vol. 14 No. 3/4, 1995, pp. 288-92.

28 Becker, C. and Olsen, M. D., "Exploring the relationship between heterogeneity and generic management trends in hospitality

Richard Teare
Hospitality operations:
patterns in management,
service improvement and
business performance

organizations", *International Journal of Hospitality Management,* Vol. 14 No. 1, 1995, pp. 39-52.

29 Collier, P. and Gregory, A., "Strategic management accounting: a UK hotel sector case study", *International Journal of Contemporary Hospitality Management,* Vol. 7 No. 1, 1995, pp. 16-21.

30 Burgess, C., Hampton, A., Price, L. and Roper, A., "International hotel groups: what makes them successful?", *International Journal of Contemporary Hospitality Management,* Vol. 7 No. 2/3, 1995, pp. 74-80.

31 Ogden, S., "Strategy, structure and employee relations: lessons from compulsory competitive tendering", *International Journal of Contemporary Hospitality Management,* Vol. 7 No. 2/3, 1995, pp. 36-41.

32 Royle, T., "Corporate versus societal culture: a comparative study of McDonald's in Europe", *International Journal of Contemporary Hospitality Management,* Vol. 7 No. 2/3, 1995, pp. 52-6.

33 Moutinho, L., McDonagh, P., Peris, S. M. and Bigne, E., "The future development of the hotel sector: an international comparison", *International Journal of Contemporary Hospitality Management,* Vol. 7 No. 4, 1995, pp. 10-15.

34 Ayala, H., "Ecoresort: a 'green' masterplan for the international resort industry", *International Journal of Hospitality Management,* Vol. 14 No. 3/4, 1995, pp. 351-74.

35 Khan, H., Seng, C. F. and Cheong, W. K., "The social impact of tourism in Singapore", *Service Industries Journal,* Vol. 9 No. 3, 1989, pp. 357-83.

36 Olokesusi, F., "An assessment of hotels in Abeokuta, Nigeria and its implications for tourists", *International Journal of Hospitality Management,* Vol. 9 No. 2, 1990, pp. 125-34.

37 Gibbons, J. D. and Fish, M., "Indonesia's international tourism: a shifting industry in Bali", *International Journal of Hospitality Management,* Vol. 8 No. 1, 1989, pp. 63-70.

38 Fish, M. and Gibbons, J. D., "Mexico's devaluations and changes in net foreign exchange receipts from tourism", *International Journal of Hospitality Management,* Vol. 10 No. 1, 1991, pp. 73-80.

39 Robinson, G. "Tourism and tourism policy in the European Community: an overview", *International Journal of Hospitality Management,* Vol. 12 No. 1, 1993, pp. 12-20.

40 Kim, C. Y. and Olsen, M. D., "A framework for the identification of political environmental issues faced by multinational hospitality chains in newly industrialized countries in Asia", *International Journal of Hospitality Management,* Vol. 12 No. 2, 1993, pp. 163-74.

41 Uysal, M., McDonald, C. D. and Marton, B. S., "Australian visitors to US national parks and natural areas", *International Journal of Contemporary Hospitality Management,* Vol. 6 No. 3, 1994, pp. 18-24.

42 Edvardsson, B., "Service breakdowns: a study of critical incidents in an airline", *International Journal of Service Industry Management,* Vol. 3 No. 4, 1992, pp. 17-29.

43 Armistead, C. G., "Service operations strategy: a framework for matching the service operations task and the service delivery system", *International Journal of Service Industry Management,* Vol. 1 No. 2, 1990, pp. 6-16.

44 Harris, P. J., "An approach to financial planning using computer spreadsheets", *International Journal of Hospitality Management,* Vol. 10 No. 1, 1991, pp. 127-36.

45 Lockwood, A. and Guerrier, Y., "Flexible working in the hospitality industry: current strategies and future potential", *International Journal of Contemporary Hospitality Management,* Vol. 1 No. 1, 1989, pp. 11-16.

46 Luckock, S. "Flexible working practices for women returners", *International Journal of Contemporary Hospitality Management,* Vol. 3 No. 3, 1991, pp. 4-9.

47 Silvestro, R., Johnston, R., Fitzgerald, L. and Voss, C., "Quality measurement in service industries", *International Journal of Service Industry Management,* Vol. 1 No. 2, 1989, pp. 54-66.

48 Brownell, J., "Hospitality managers' communication practices", *International Journal of Hospitality Management,* Vol. 9 No. 3, 1990, pp. 191-205.

49 Ineson, E. M. and Brown, S. H. P., "The use of biodata for hotel employee selection", *International Journal of Contemporary Hospitality Management,* Vol. 4 No. 2, 1992, pp. 8-12.

Managing environmental change: insights from researchers and practitioners

John T. Bowen

Research Director (North America), Worldwide Hospitality and Tourism Trends, William F. Harrah College of Hotel Administration, University of Nevada, Las Vegas, USA

Analyses the articles published in the *FIU Hospitality Review* during a seven-year period from 1989-1995. Identifies seven main themes: people and organizations; marketing; environmental change; total quality management and strategy; education; financial analysis and accounting practice; tourism and technology. Summarizes by highlighting the linkages between the themes and the related sub-themes.

Introduction

The purpose of this review is to identify themes and their related sub-themes of articles published in the *FIU Hospitality Review* between 1989 and 1995. Florida International University publishes the *Review*. The *FIU Hospitality Review* publishes both empirical research and conceptual articles. The authors in the *Review* include both hospitality managers and educators. The *Review's* articles maintain a practical focus.

The review identifies seven main themes. They are:
1 people and organizations;
2 marketing;
3 environmental change, total quality management and strategy;
4 education;
5 financial analysis and accounting practice;
6 tourism; and
7 technology.

The article provides a discussion of each theme and sub-theme. At the end of the discussion a summary table of the theme is provided. A summary table and a figure showing the linkage between the sub-themes is provided at the end of the article.

Theme 1: people and organizations

Hospitality managers are increasingly realizing the value of effective human resource management, as almost one third of the *Review's* articles related to people and organizations. There are 28 sub-themes (see Table I) grouped into five sub-headings as follows: employee recruitment and retention; employee competences and training; leadership, management style, and employee motivation; employee costs and problems; and ethics and discrimination in the workplace.

Employee recruitment and retention

Articles in this group deal with the labour shortage facing hospitality firms in many areas of the USA. The first set of articles focuses on attracting employees. Several articles within this group look at attracting employees from non-traditional sources. Annath and DeMicco[1] (Table I) state that a traditional source of labour for the hospitality industry, the 16-24 year old, will decline over the next 20 years. The 55 and older group has doubled, as a percentage of the population, from 10 per cent to 20 per cent since 1900 and will continue to grow. They also report that 20 per cent of Americans return to work after retiring. Meier[2] cites that older workers, working mothers, and the disabled are all sources of employees often overlooked by the hospitality industry. Jones *et al.*[3] report on the use of economically disadvantaged people. They state that this group can be a good source of employees. Additionally, their employment removes them from state benefit rolls, creates the opportunity for a new life for the chronically unemployed, and can be a source of government funding for the business employing the economically disadvantaged. Rainero and Chon[4] suggest marketing techniques be applied to human resource management in order to attract employees.

The second set of articles relates to retaining employees. Barrows[5] states that employee turnover is recognized as one of the central problems facing hospitality managers. Not only is employee turnover expensive, but other employee behaviour that may precede turnover is also costly. This behaviour includes tardiness, absenteeism, and diminished enthusiasm towards the job. Barrows recommends that managers get to know and understand their employees. Once they have knowledge of their employees, they can address their needs through job redesign, reassignment, compensation, and other tools used to enrich the employees' situation. George[6] states that turnover in the restaurant costs $2,500 per employee. His research validates Barrows' claim that managers can influence turnover. George found managers could control 47.8 per cent of the factors which lead to voluntary separation of restaurant employees. Cantrell and Sarabakhsh[7] found that employee compensation, training, and chance for promotion were three factors that affected employee turnover. These researchers all realize that employee turnover is a major problem in the hospitality industry. It is not enough to attract good employees. Managers must also develop ways to retain employees.

Table I
People and organizations

Authors	Focus	Sub-theme
Ananth and DeMicco[1]	Investigates the use of older workers as an alternative source of labour to alleviate the labour shortage in the hospitality industry	Older workers
Meier[2]	Investigates the use of older workers, working mothers, and the disabled as an alternative source of labour to alleviate the labour shortage in the hospitality industry	Older workers
Jones, *et al.*[3]	Reports on the implementation and benefits of hiring economically disadvantaged persons	Economically disadvantaged employees
Rainero and Chon[4]	Explains how the labour crisis is affecting the hospitality industry and makes suggestions about how the application of marketing techniques to human resource management will help attract quality employees	Internal marketing
Barrows[5]	Investigates the determinants and predictors of employee turnover	Employee turnover
George[6]	Reports the results of an exploratory study to determine the reasons why employees voluntarily leave their jobs	Employee turnover
Cantrel and Sarabakhsh[[7]	Assesses the relationship between job and management characteristics and turnover of employees	Employee turnover
Van Dyke and Strick[8]	Investigates the process of recruitment selection, and retention of managers in US restaurant and hotel chains	Employee retention
Williams and Hunter[9]	Explores the recruitment and retention implications of promoting junior level managers to senior positions	Internal promotion
Fulford and Wanger[10]	Explores and gives recommendations on how hospitality jobs can be made more attractive to younger workers	Younger workers
Altman and Brothers[11]	Examines factors affecting hospitality college graduates' career longevity, their likes and dislikes about employment, and their reasons for continuing employment or leaving the hospitality industry	Graduates' career longevity
Warner[12]	Investigates the education, training and development needs for recreational food service managers	Incentives for productivity
O'Halloran and Wong[14]	Investigates the skills and competences of theme park managers and provides suggestions based on the results of the study	Employee competences
O'Halloran and Wong[13]	Investigates the skills and competences of US National Park managers and provides suggestions based on the results of of the study	Employee competences
Kavanaugh and Ninemeier[15]	Explores the use of interactive video as a training tool and discusses its advantages of other training devices	Interactive video
Harris[16]	Explores how to break down the barriers that are preventing multimedia from being used in hospitality training	Multimedia
Crafts and Sanders[17]	Surveys managers to gain their perceptions of the value of alcohol server training programmes	Alcohol server training
O'Halloran[18]	Reviews and provides critical commentary of the models and approaches for training effective managers	Management training
Crafts[19]	Investigates managers' perceptions of alcohol server training programmes	Alcohol server training
Lynn[20]	Looks at the relationship between training preparation and training methods utilized by restaurant managers	Training methods
Breiter *et al.*[21]	Surveys corporate directors of human resources on specific activities and tasks associated with experiential learning in the guest services areas of hotels	Experiential learning

(Continued)

Table I

Authors	Focus	Sub-theme
O'Halloran[22]	Presents a case study to train managers in the skills needed to handle crisis management	Crisis management
Fisher[23]	Comments on how the rapid growth of the food service industry has redefined the role of the manager	Management style
Kent[24]	Reports on a paradigm shift in management style, vanguard management	Management style
Cichy et al.[25]	Reports on a study that investigated the traits of effective hospitality leaders, managers' perceptions of the keys to effective leadership and the qualities leaders must possess	Leadership
Goll[26]	Investigates differences between what workers want from their jobs and what managers perceive workers want	Employee motivation
Meyer and Schroeder[27]	Examines why hospitality employees are not rewarded for productivity	Incentives for productivity
George[28]	Discusses how managers must be an effective link between the formal organization and the employees of the organization	Communication
Lundberg[29]	Reports on the results of surveys of students and managers to show patterned differences in work ideologies and discusses the implications of these differences	Work ideologies
Cichy et al.[30]	Reports on a survey that investigates what Japanese lodging industry presidents and CEOs think are essential leadership qualities	Leadership
Ralston[31]	Reports on the effect of the manager-customer relationship in decision making by managers	Manager-customer relationship
Eade and Jonak[32]	Investigates what managers can do to control drugs in the workplace	Drugs in the workplace
Eade[33]	Identifies a number of problem indicators and makes recommendations for resolving the drug abuse problem	Drugs in the workplace
Silfies and DeMicco[34]	Presents an assessment of the substance abuse problems in the workplace and a review of procedures for management of substance abuse in the workplace	Drugs in the workplace
Ghiselli and Ismail[35]	Investigates whether certain policies and procedures were more effective than others in reducing employee theft	Employee theft
Ladki[36]	Discusses strategies to help employers reduce health care costs, increase employee productivity, and improve job satisfaction	Health care costs
Chandraesekar and Cichy[37]	Develops a model to track and quantify the costs of absenteeism in service industries	Absenteeism
Gregg and Johnson[38]	Examines if discriminatory practices against equally well-trained, qualified and experienced female middle managers affects their perception of career growth when compared to male counterparts	Gender-based discrimination
Brownwell[39]	Explores female managers' perceptions of the career-related challenges they confront in hospitality environments reports on the concerns of women managers	Gender-based discrimination
Schmidgall[40]	Reports on lodging managers' reactions to a number of scenarios testing ethical situations	Ethics

Employee competences and training

The articles in this sub-theme can be categorized into two groups. The first group relates to competences and skills needed to perform jobs. The second group of articles investigates the effectiveness of training techniques and methods. Warner[12] uses a panel of experts to prioritize a previously developed list of 30 knowledge competences and 30 skill competences needed for managers of recreational food facilities. This type of facility includes sports stadiums, amusement parks, and convention centres. Warner states that many hospitality training programmes treat food as a segment and do not address the need of specialized segments within the food service sector. Warner's study puts forth the argument that specialized segments of the hospitality industry have distinct needs. Managers must implement needs assessment and use the results to develop specialized training programmes. O'Halloran and Wong[13,14] continue this theme by investigating the skills needed by theme park managers and US National Park managers. One of the implications of these studies is that hospitality training programmes will become more focused.

Kavanaugh and Ninemeir[15] state that interactive video allows employees to work through realistic situations at their own pace. They claim that this type of training has no negative impact on guests. Harris[16] states that multimedia has been proved to increase the efficiency and effectiveness of training programmes and reduce the cost of delivery. While these authors extol the use of technology in training, they state that the would-be users must become knowledgeable about multimedia choices and understand how to incorporate technology effectively into training programmes.

Leadership, management style, and employee motivation

This sub-theme looks at management and leadership issues, trying to discover how managers can effectively motivate and lead their employees. Fisher[23] states that managers must be more receptive to new ideas, new contingencies, and new technologies. He argues that they need to understand internal marketing, total quality management and local store marketing. Kent[24], like Fisher, discusses the changing role of a manager. He states that managers must realize that their decisions affect a host of stakeholders and they must learn to balance the needs of the stakeholders. These researchers hold that the roles of a manager are dynamic and managers must keep up with their changing environment.

Cichy *et al.*[25] surveyed lodging and food-service executives asking them to rate 24 leadership attributes. The qualities that were recognized as the most important are having strong values, being visionary, staying informed, communication and perseverance. Goll[26] studied motivation at the unit level. He found that the supervisor's views of what employees want from their jobs differed from what employees really wanted. Goll states that managers must be empathetic to employee needs, and that without this understanding managers will have a difficult time motivating their employees. The skills required to lead a company and manage a business unit are a continuing theme of research and it is likely that this area will be of interest to both managers and researchers in the future.

Employee costs and problems

An interesting and important sub-theme is employee costs and problems. Eade and Jonak[32], Eade[33] and Silfies and DeMicco[34] discuss the problems of drugs in the workplace. Eade and Jonak state that one in four workers knows someone who uses illegal drugs on the job. They also claim that drug use costs US businesses $100 billion a year. These authors emphasize that managers must become knowledgeable in drug detection, counselling, and treatment resolution. Ghiselli and Ismail[35] discuss another problem often related to drug use, employee theft. These researchers found that 2 per cent of sales in the restaurant business are lost to employee theft. As drug use increases, employee theft will also increase. These topics address relatively new problems faced by managers.

Another growing concern of managers, as well as employees, is health care costs. Ladki[36] argues that health care costs can be reduced by making your employees more healthy. Many corporations have initiated wellness programmes. The author states that these programmes including dietary counselling, exercise, and behavior modification should be implemented in the food service sector. Research has shown that obese employees are more prone to disease and health-related absences than non-obese employees. Ladki's article reflects the growing trend of partnershipping. In this case the employer is providing the employee with health club benefits, dietary consultants, and medical counselling. The employee becomes healthier as a result of these alliances, and the employer's health care costs and employee absenteeism rate is reduced.

Ethics and discrimination in the workplace

The final sub-theme in this area is ethics and discrimination. Gregg and Johnson[38] and Brownell[39] investigate gender-based discrimination. Brownell looks into reasons why women who are now better represented in low and mid-level management positions are not well represented in top management positions. Brownell cites a lack of role models and the lack of access to networks that often open doors to top management positions. Brownell is optimistic about the

John T. Bowen
*Managing environmental
change: insights from
researchers and practitioners*

future for women. Women in top positions must learn to serve as role models for women in mid-management positions. Schmidgall[40] makes a useful contribution by providing a number of scenarios which can be used to gain insight into the values held by employees or used for teaching ethics.

Theme 2: marketing

This theme area has 17 sub-themes (see Table II) and the commentary uses the following subheadings: segmentation; product attributes and product selection; promotion; and marketing information.

Segmentation
Two articles give an overview of the segmentation process. Nicholls and Roslow[41] provide an overview of segmentation and its application to the hotel sector. The segmentation process involves three steps, market segmentation, choosing the target market(s) and positioning. Dickson[42] explains how carnival cruise lines successfully positioned themselves as the "fun ship".

Five recent articles, from the autumn of 1992 on, discuss the senior market. Pederson[43] states that in the next 30 years the number of people older than 50 will grow by 74 per cent, while the number of people under 50 will grow by only 1 per cent. It is estimated that by the year 2030 seniors will account for close to half of all air travel and hotel rooms in the USA. She states that people currently 60-80 grew up during the depression and tend to be conservative. These characteristics have given some managers a poor image of seniors as customers. Pederson states that the new seniors will be more active and more willing to try different cuisine. Pederson and DeMicco[44] and Harris and West[45] discuss what seniors seek in restaurants. Gustin and Weaver[46] discuss what seniors look for in hotels.

Product attributes and product selection
A number of articles look at the importance of product attributes to the consumer. These articles show the desire of managers to fine tune their operations and to invest in attributes that will create value for their market segment. Evans and Murrman[48] investigate the value created by personal care amenities as part of the lodging product. Their findings suggest that at least 75 per cent of hotel guests considered PCA packages important product attributes and would select a hotel based on the reputation of its PCA package. Kapoor[49] found that taste is

much more important to young adults than nutrition. Since fats usually add taste to food products, it appears that sacrificing taste to reduce fat will not be a winning formula in the near term for the younger fast food market. This has been validated as McDonald's has eliminated their low fat hamburger and Taco Bell has scraped their reduced fat items. Cai and Ninemeier[S0] explain how Chinese hotels have adapted serving styles to fit the tourist's expectations.

Promotion
The articles on promotion covered a variety of issues. Dienhart and Lefever[55] looked at the use of marquees as a promotional tool. Barrows *et al.*[56] found that favourable restaurant reviews had a positive effect on potential customers. They also found that a negative review could have a devastating impact on a restaurant. Only 2 per cent of the respondents said they were likely to go to a restaurant that received a negative review, while 89 per cent indicated they would be unlikely to visit the restaurant.

Marketing information
This sub-theme dealt with gaining and using marketing information. Gregg[59] looks at research methodology and specifically the development and implementation of a survey instrument. Davidson[60] cites the need for primary research. Vladimir[61] and Chon and Whelihan[62] discuss the need for information which the dynamic environment creates. The authors state that resort marketers must understand changing demographics and economic conditions in order to create value for their guests.

Theme 3: environmental change, total quality management and strategy

The third theme has 13 sub-themes (see Table III) dealing with environmental trends and strategic issues. This theme is divided into four sub-headings: environment and change; environmental issues; total quality management; and strategy.

Environment and change
This sub-theme looks at the impact the environment has on industry segments and markets. Harnson[63] claims that the restaurant sector operates in a rapidly changing environment and, because of this, restaurant operators cope with change. Using the restaurant sector and other examples Harrison provides a framework for managing change. Muller and Woods[64]

Table II
Marketing

Authors	Focus	Sub-theme
Nicholls and Roslow[41]	Analyses the segmentation movement in the hotel industry and compares it with the segmentation of consumer goods	Segmentation
Dickson[42]	Presents Carnival cruise lines positioning philosophy	Positioning
Pederson[43]	Discusses the future senior travel market and provides recommendations for attracting and servicing this group	Senior market
Pederson and DeMicco[44]	Present strategies to attract and enhance the dining experiences for the senior market segment	Senior market
Harris and West[45]	Researches the service expectations of the active mature restaurant segment	Senior market
Gustin and Weaver[46]	Investigates the underlying dimensions that exist for the mature individual with regard to the selection criteria for lodging used for pleasure travel	Senior market
Pederson[47]	Discusses the similarities and differences of the current and future senior markets and offers recommendations for meeting the needs of this segment	Senior market
Evans and Murrmann[48]	Investigates the importance to the guest of personal care amenities and if amenities impacts the hotel selection decision	Personal care amenities
Kapoor[49]	Investigates the importance of fast food restaurants having nutritious menu items available for young adults	Nutritious menu items
Cai and Ninemeier[50]	Researches how Chinese hotels have adapted serving styles to fit tourists' wants with minimal compromise to culinary traditions	Product adaptation
Nusbaum[51]	Presents a system for improving guest satisfaction through the design of lodging facilities	Product design
Morcos et al.[52]	Explores the customer perceptions of speed of service, courtesy and and quality of good at fast food restaurants	Product attributes
Strick et al.[53]	Discusses the role "hospitality" plays in restaurant service	Service
Holland and McCool[54]	Examines cross-cultural cuisine to determine if it is a trend or a fad and discusses catalysts that promoted or hindered its trend/fad status	Cross-cultural cuisine
Dienhart and Lefever[55[	Examines the use and misuse of marquees as a promotional tool	Marquees
Barrow et al.[56]	Researches the role that restaurant reviews play in the consumers purchase decision process	Restaurant reviews
Strate[57]	Discusses the implications of new laws and recent court cases that opened up advertising in the gaming sector	Advertising
Smith et al.[58]	Examines whether printed menu theories and techniques can be applied, with the same results, to a computer menu screen	Menu design
Gregg[59]	Discusses how to design questions, construct the survey, and watch for errors in conducting the research so that the results secured advance scientific inquiry	Survey development
Davidson[60]	Reports on the need for primary market research	Primary market research
Vladimir[61]	Discusses how changing customer bases, changing technology and changing ways of motivating and managing employees will affect marketing	Marketing intelligence
Chon and Whelichas[62]	Investigates how environmental changes will impact the marketing of resorts	Marketing intelligence

John T. Bowen
*Managing environmental
change: insights from
researchers and practitioners*

Table III
Environmental change, total quality management and strategy

Authors	Focus	Sub-theme
Harrison[63]	Discusses how to evaluate and act on a management change plan beginning with a total understanding and knowledge of the environment	Management change
Muller and Woods[64]	Presents a study of ten years in the life of three restaurant markets	Environmental change
Parsa and Khan[65]	Gives an analysis of the current and emerging trends in the quick service restaurant sector	Trend analysis
Chon and Huo[66]	Identifies the perceptions of conference centre managers of future trends and provides them with environmental information so they can plan better for the future	Environmental information
Welsh and Swerdlow[67]	Looks at how the internationalization of the hospitality industry has created opportunities and challenges in the Russian Federation	Internationalization of the hospitality industry
Kotschevar[68]	Discusses what the food service industry can and should do to meet the nutritional needs of consumers better, as an increasing percentage of consumers food is supplied by restaurants	Nutrition
Ahmed and Krohn[69]	Examines the impact of hotel taxes, reviews hotel tax rates in cities across the USA and proposes a process by which hotel tax revenues can be disbursed equitably and efficiently	Hotel tax
Myers and Urdang[70]	Discusses from both a legal and managerial perspective, one of the least known dangers associated with borrowing, lender liability	Lender liability
Jaffe et al.[71]	Looks at managers' attitudes and practices towards solid waste disposal	Solid waste disposal
Gaston[72]	Reports on a court case which ruled that if certain requirements were met a restaurant could be trademarked	Trade dress
Breiter and Fried-Kline[73]	Looks at the process of total quality management in the hotel sector	Total quality management
Welsh[74]	Discusses how quality problems have been compounded in the fast food sector and how quality control can lead to success	Quality control
Vladimir[75]	Reports on how a cruise line implemented a total quality management programme	Total quality management
Haywood[76]	Identifies the principles of strategy that corporate strategists could utilize in testing their strategic theories, concepts and plans	Strategy

provide an analysis of restaurant failures over a ten-year period in three different markets. They state "while generally attributed to operator mismanagement, [failure] may rely more on environmental conditions than individual management practices". The authors imply that good management may not always be able to overcome negative environmental conditions. Parsa and Khan[65] look at how environmental changes have affected the quick service food sector. Chon and Huo[66] provide an environmental analysis of the conference centre business. Welsh and Swerdlow[67] look at how the globalization of business and the fall of the Soviet Union have created opportunities for the hospitality industry in the Russian Federation.

Environmental issues

This sub-theme investigates specific issues that have developed because of changes in the business environment. A hotel tax on room sales is often seen by local politicians as a way to raise taxes from visitors and lessen the burden on the local population, the voters. Ahmed and Krohn[69] examine the impact of hotel taxes in cities across the USA. Most studies show that a small increase has little impact on demand; however, in New York a percentage tax in double digits was found to have a negative impact on demand. The authors cite one study that found that tourists were more price sensitive than was previously realized. Ahmed and Krohn take the position that a small tax, where the proceeds are used to benefit the tourist industry,

John T. Bowen
*Managing environmental
change: insights from
researchers and practitioners*

can be useful. However, they caution that the hospitality industry must monitor the tax legislation to make sure the proceeds will benefit the tourist industry.

Myers and Urdang[70] discuss a change in the legal environment, lender liability, and the implications of this change for the hospitality industry. The authors state that senior management should be aware that in certain circumstances lenders can be held legally responsible to third parties for the wrongful act or omissions of the borrower. Jaffe *et al.*[71] state that the USA is one of the leading producers of solid waste in the world. Landfills for this waste are quickly disappearing, resulting in the disposal of solid waste being ranked as one the most important environmental problems faced by public and private decision makers. The authors research current practices and provide recommendations for managers. Gaston[72] reports on the implications of a recent court case involving trade-dress in the restaurant sector.

Total quality management
The concept of total quality management in service industries is still evolving. Vladimir[75] investigates how quality is achieved on one of the top rated cruise lines, Seabourn. Breiter and Fried-Kline[73] cite the lack of research on what hotels are actually accomplishing in terms of total quality management as one of the justifications for their study. In their study the authors investigate and report on the best practices of the hotels in the USA known for their total quality management systems.

Strategy
The fourth sub-theme is strategy. Only one article was published on overall strategy during this six-year period. Haywood[76] puts forth ten principles of strategy that corporate strategists could utilize in testing their strategic theories, concepts and plans.

Theme 4: education

The fourth theme has 11 sub-themes (see Table IV) categorized into four sub-headings: curriculum and accreditation; courses; technology and teaching methods; and placement of graduates.

Curriculum and accreditation
The Council of Hotel, Restaurant, and Institutional Educators (CHRIE) formed an accrediting commission in 1989. Williams[77] reports on some of the issues the accrediting commission will have to address and, it is hoped, clarify. These issues are: who is in charge of

the curriculum content of hospitality education programmes – industry or educators? Is this really a profession in need of an accreditation process? Are hospitality educators in the business of training or educating? Following a trend seen earlier in the people and organizations sub-theme, O'Halloran[78] discusses the need for a curriculum designed to meet the needs of a particular industry group (state tourism managers).

Courses
The second area looks at the addition of specific courses to curricula. Casado[80] calls for leadership courses to be added to hospitality curricula. Casado *et al.*[81] discuss the importance of having ethics courses added to curricula. Again, the areas of ethics and leadership are two areas mentioned in theme 1, people and organizations. The educational issues raised by educators are similar to the training issues we see emerging in the industry.

Technology and teaching methods
Kassavana[82] advocates software which uses short case studies to instruct students. He claims computer aided learning can serve as powerful catalysts for creative thinking and problem solving. In a later volume, Kassavana[83] discusses a range of technological platforms that can be used to support education, including audiographics and virtual reality simulation. He predicts that the technology will extend the boundaries of the traditional classroom. Breiter[84] and Breiter *et al.*[85] look at experiential learning.

Placement of graduates
Every university has two major clients – its students and those who hire its students – thus creating value for the university's degree. Van Dyke and Montgomery[86] look at the recruiters' perceptions of career fairs as an information source for both students and perspective employers. Jones *et al.*[87] found that the profile of college recruiters had not changed significantly between 1983 and 1992, with one notable exception – gender. Women had made inroads towards achieving equality. Altman and Brothers[88] look at why graduates quit or stay with jobs after they graduate.

Theme 5: financial analysis and accounting practice

This area is made up of 11 sub-themes (see Table V). The sub-themes are divided into three subheadings: accounting practice; financial management; and financial statements and annual reports.

John T. Bowen
*Managing environmental
change: insights from
researchers and practitioners*

Table IV
Education

Authors	Focus	Sub-theme
Williams[77]	Discusses hospitality education in light of the CHRIE accreditation process	Accreditation
O'Halloran[78]	Discusses curricular for the programme in tourism management education based on a survey of state tourism directors	Curricula for directors
Chesser and Ellis[79]	Reports on hospitality programme administrators views regarding the current and preferred location for the teaching of the common core areas of hospitality administration	Core curriculum
Casado[80]	Investigates leadership courses in hospitality curricula	Leadership course
Casado *et al.*[82]	Shows the importance of having ethics as part of the curriculum by comparing perceptions of ethics of students who have taken an ethics courses with the industry managers	Ethics course
Kasavana[82]	Discusses the relevance of specially designed computer-based courseware for the hospitality curriculum	Computer-based courseware
Kasavana[83]	Discusses the application to hospitality education of technological platforms for multimedia instructional courseware, distance learning through audio graphics and virtual reality simulation	Multimedia instructional courseware
Breiter[84]	Reports on student perceptions of three commonly stated goals of experiential learning programmes: the application of classroom studies, technical training and management development	Experiential learning programmes
Breiter *et al.*[85]	Reports on a survey of corporate directors of human resources on specific activities and tasks associated with experiential learning in the guest services areas of hotels	Experiential learning programmes
Van Dyke and Montgomery[86]	Reports on recruiters perceptions of career fairs based on a survey	Career fairs
Jones *et al.*[87]	Investigates changes in college recruiters and gives implications for college students going through the interviewing process	College recruiters
Altman and Brothers[88]	Investigates graduates' reasons for continuing employment in the hospitality industry and reasons for exiting the industry	Employment longevity of graduates

Accounting practice
This sub-theme contains articles that look at specific accounting issues. Tarras and Schmidgall[89] look at how the industry deals with tip allocation. Tarras[90] gives insight into how firms can minimize their chances of having independent contractors reclassified as employees. The consequences of having independent contractors reclassified include paying income tax withholding and social security, without any right to recover these payments from the employee. VanLoenen and Holland[91] also provide tax information. These authors discuss how personal liability may arise for unpaid corporate payroll tax.

Financial management
The third sub-theme is financial management. With the exception of one article, the articles in this group deal with longitudinal

and case studies. Tavlin *et al.*[93] look at the financial failure of hospitality companies and provide lessons to be learned from each case. Moncarz[94] analyses the performance of lodging firms from 1987 to 1990. She states that most recovered fairly quickly from the crash of 1987, but that they did not recover quickly from the mini-crash of 1989. She provides a number of financial reasons why lodging sticks failed to rebound in late 1989 and early 1990. Moncarz[95] also provides an analysis of leveraged buy outs.

Financial statements and annual reports
In 1989 there were two articles on the use of financial statements and annual reports as management tools. Schmidgall[97] analyses how managers perceive the importance and usefulness ratios. Moncarz[98] provides

John T. Bowen
*Managing environmental
change: insights from
researchers and practitioners*

Table V

Financial analysis and accounting practice

Authors	Focus	Sub-theme
Tarras and Schmidgall[89]	Discusses the results of a survey researching how the commercial food industry sector deals with tip allocation	Tip allocation
Tarras[90]	Provides planning tips so hospitality firms can minimize their chances of having independent contractors reclassified as employees	Independent contractors
Vall Loenen and Holland[91]	Discusses where personal liability may arise for unpaid corporate payroll taxes	Payroll tax
Damitio and Kagley[92]	Reports on descriptive research gathered from controllers in the hospitality industry	Practices of controllers
Tavlin et al.[93]	Studies the basic reasons underlying failed ideas while presenting a study of several hospitality chains that have experienced varying degrees of financial failure	Causes of financial failure
Moncarz[94]	Studies how selected lodging firms have fared since the summer rally of 1987	Stock performance
Moncarz[95]	Examines major developments affecting leveraged buyouts over the past five years and addresses their future implications	Leveraged buyout
Schmidgall[96]	Discusses research findings on how the 25 largest contract food service management firms organize and implement the budgeting process	Budgeting
Schmidgall[97]	Analyses the results of two surveys designed to rank the degree of importance and usefulness of these ratios to several user groups	Financial ratios
Moncarz[98]	Focuses on the examination and understanding of annual reports, suggests guidelines for using them in decision making, and discusses recent developments affecting these reports	Annual reports

guidelines for using annual reports in decision making.

Theme 6: tourism

This area has eight sub-themes (see Table VI) clustered into three sub-headings: tourism and the environment; tourism research; and tourism destinations.

Tourism and the environment
Rymer[99] states that the critical factor which differentiates ecotourism from other more traditional forms of tourism is the conscious effort to minimize tourism's negative environmental impacts. He claims there is a growing demand for ecotourism. O'Halloran[100] examines the environmental impact of national park concessions, while Yu[101] looks at developing marine tourism in the Red Sea.

Tourism research
Two of the research studies look at the needs for tourism research. O'Halloran and Holecek[102] reports on the research needs of the tourism professional. Sun and Uysal[103] investigate the research needs of the theme

park dusiness. The other article in this sub-theme, O'Halloran and Holecek[104] look at the need for collaborative efforts between private and public organizations.

Tourism destinations
Two studies examine tourism destinations. Milman[105] looks at Floridians as a potential market for Canada. Hobson and Ko[106] investigate the changing expectations of inbound tourists to Hong Kong.

Theme 7: technology

The technology theme has seven sub-themes (see Table VII) divided into two sub-themes: information systems and teleconferencing. Kasavana[107] states that intuitive, object-oriented, and wire technologies will have a positive impact on information systems. Howey and Savage[108] present some alternatives to using technology to increase information processing. Ford et al.[109] give advice for setting up an information system. Singh and Chon[113] were the only authors to look at issues other than information systems. They discuss how hotels can profit from teleconferencing.

John T. Bowen
*Managing environmental
change: insights from
researchers and practitioners*

Table VI
Tourism

Authors	Focus	Sub-theme
Rymer[99]	Examines factors involved in the growth of the US ecotourism market in order to project the growth of this market during the 1990s	Ecotourism
O'Halloran[100]	Examines the relationship of national park concessions and the environments in which they operate	National park concessions
Yu[101]	Recommendations are presented to develop coastal and marine tourism in the Red Sea area	Marine tourism – Red Sea
O'Halloran and Holecek[102]	Reports on the research needs of tourism professionals including; data used and needed, the types of decisions made, and where data are obtained	Research needs
Sun and Uysal[103]	Investigates and identifies research topics for the theme park business	Theme park research need
O'Halloran and Holecek[104]	Discusses the need for a collaborative effort between private and public organizations to establish a high quality tourism database	Collaborative research efforts between private and public organizations
Milman[105]	Reports on a survey of Floridians as to their attitudes towards Canada as a tourism destination	Destination marketing
Hobson and Ko[106]	Explores the changes in the tourism market for Hong Kong and the implications for the Hong Kong hotel industry	Tourism markets

Table VII
Technology

Authors	Focus	Sub-theme
Kasavana[107]	Looks at how intuitive, object-oriented and wireless technologies will impact the hospitality industry	Intuitive, object-oriented, and wireless technologies
Howey and Savage[108]	Uses a theoretical framework to illustrate alternative mechanisms that can be used to co-ordinate and control hotel operations	Alternative information systems
Ford *et al.*[109]	Presents and overview of how to implement an information system	Information systems
Collins[110]	Discusses those factors which are critical to POS system selection for table service restaurants	POS system
Jensen[111]	Examines the pros and cons of outsourcing to help the hospitality industry determine if this is a business practice to be considered	Outsourcing information systems
Collins[112]	Reports the results of a survey of corporate executives designed to assess how technology is affecting their organizations	Impact of technology on organizations
Singh and Chon[113]	Discusses the factors that spurred the growth of teleconferencing and provides suggestions for taking advantage of the technology	Teleconferencing

Conclusions

This analysis has brought together a number of different issues through a thematic overview. One common thread through all of the themes is the impact of the environment on the business. Authors continue to tell readers that the hospitality industry's ability to change lags behind other industries. Yet, some advances occurring in the hospitality industry indicate that it is catching up, if not passing some other industries. The hospitality industry is going through a period of unprecedented change. A number of trends and challenges were identified from the analysis of the *FIU Hospitality Review*. They are reported below and summarized in Table VIII and Figure 1.

- The labour shortage is forcing smart firms to develop marketing-like approaches to attract and retain good employees. Partner-shipping with employees will become essential.
- As segments of the industry become more specialized, the competences enabling one to be an effective manager in a specific segment will be valued.
- Training is headed towards interactive, self-paced, training methods.

John T. Bowen
*Managing environmental
change: insights from
researchers and practitioners*

Table VIII
The *FIU Hospitality Review:* a thematic perspective

Themes	Sub-themes	Observations
Theme 1: **people and organizations**	Older workers; economically disadvantaged employees; younger workers; internal marketing; employee turnover	The labour shortage is forcing smart firms to develop marketing like approaches to attract and retain good employees. Partnershipping with employees will become essential
	Employee competences; interactive video; multimedia	As segments of the industry become more specialized, the competences enabling one to be an effective manager in a specific segment will be valued
		Training is headed towards interactive, self-paced, training methods
	Management style; leadership; employee motivation; incentive for productivity; communication	To retain employees managers will have to become leaders who can motivate employees
Theme 2: **marketing**	Segmentation; positioning; senior market	Companies are seeking out market segments that will create value for the company and for which they can create value. All customers are no longer considered equal
		The segmentation process will be used in human resource management to select employees and to customize training and education
	Personal care amenities, product adoption; product design; product attributes; service	Companies will need to fine tune their marketing mix to create value for the desired segments
	Restaurant reviews; advertising; menu design	Communicating with the market will be more important as firms move towards one-to-one marketing
	Survey development; primary research; marketing intelligence	Marketing research will be used more frequently as companies work to stay close to their customer
Theme 3: **environmental change** **total quality management** **and strategy**	Management change: environmental change: internationalization of the hotel sector; hotel tax; lender liability	Managers need to continue to be proactive to environmental changes
Theme 4: **education**	Curricula for tourism directors	Hospitality education is moving from applied general business training and education to competence based training and education for specific industry segments
	Leadership course: ethics course	Educational institutes will need to develop new courses to fit changing industry needs
	Computer-based courseware; multimedia instructional courseware	Generation-X and beyond will require new delivery methods
Theme 5: **financial analysis and** **accounting practice**	Tip allocation; independent contractors causes of financial failure; stock performance	Companies' accounting practices and financial performance will continue to be driven by environmental changes
Theme 6: **tourism**	Ecotourism, National Park concessions, marine tourism	Tourism development, and indeed all facets of business will need to be more concerned with the environment. The environment must be viewed as a scarce resource, that must be preserved for the future
Theme 7: **technology**	Intuitive, object oriented and wireless technologies, alternative information POS system, outsourcing information systems	Companies must have integrated information systems with multiple entry points and multiple retrieval points

John T. Bowen
Managing environmental change: insights from researchers and practitioners

- To retain employees managers will have to become leaders who can motivate employees.
- Companies are seeking out market segments that will create value for the company and for which they can create value. All customers are no longer considered equal.
- The segmentation process will be used in human resource management to select employees and to customize training and education.
- Companies will need to fine tune their marketing mix to create value for the desired segments.
- Hospitality education is moving from applied general business training and education to competence-based training and education for specific industry segments.
- Tourism development, and indeed all facets of business, will need to be more concerned with the environment. The environment must be viewed as a scarce resource that must be preserved for the future.

- Companies must have integrated information systems with multiple entry points and multiple retrieval points.

References

(All the following references are from the *FIU Hospitality Reviews*)

1 Ananth, M. and DeMicco, F.J., "Strategies for tomorrow's hospitality workforce", Vol. 9 No. 1, 1991, pp. 25-38.
2 Meier, J.D., "Solutions to the hospitality industry's labour shortage", Vol. 9 No. 2, 1991, p. 78.
3 Jones, T., Fried, B. and Nazarechuk, A., "Corporate responsibility on a 'grand' scale: MGM's employment outreach program", Vol. 12 No. 2, 1994, pp. 1-12.
4 Rainero, C.J. and Chon, K.S., "Marketing approaches to human resources management in the hospitality industry", Vol. 8 No. 1, 1990, pp. 32-40.
5 Barrows, C.W., "Employee turnover: implications for hotel managers", Vol. 8 No. 1, 1990, pp. 24-31.
6 George, R.T., "Voluntary termination in restaurants: an exploratory determination of causes", Vol. 9. No. 1, 1991, pp. 59-66.
7 Cantrell, N. and Sarabakhsh, M., "Correlates of non-institutional food service turnover", Vol. 9 No. 2, 1991, pp. 52-9.
8 Van Dyke, T. and Strick, S., "Recruitment, selection and retention of managers in the hotel and restaurant industry", FIUHospitalityReview, Vol. 8 No. 1, 1990, pp. 1-9.
9 Williams, P.W. and Hunter, M., "Recruitment and retention insights for the hotel industry", Vol. 9 No. 1, 1991, pp. 51-8.
10 Fulford, M.D. and Wagner, R.J, "Making non-career jobs attractive to younger workers", Vol. 12 No. 2, 1993, pp. 71-8.
11 Altman, L.A. and Brothers, L.R., "Career longevity of hospitality graduates", Vol. 13 No. 2, 1995, pp. 77-84.
12 Warner, M., "A new look at institutional food service management", Vol. 10 No. 1, 1992, pp. 27-40.
13 O'Halloran, R.M. and Wong, S.L, "Tourism professional profile: theme park managers", Vol. 12 No. 1, 1994, pp. 59-70.
14 O'Halloran, R.M. and Wong, C.S., "Standards for tourism management success: US National Park managers", Vol. 12 No. 2, 1994, pp. 45-58.
15 Kavanaugh, R.R. and Ninemeier, J.D., "Interactive video instruction: a training tool whose time has come", Vol. 9 No. 2, 1991, pp. 1-6.
16 Harris, K.J., "Multimedia training: why some use it and some do not", Vol. 12 No. 2, 1994, p. 79.
17 Crafts, D.D. and Sanders, R.E., "Manager's perceptions of alcohol server staffing and training methods", Vol. 7 No. 1, 1989, p. 92.

Figure 1
Managing in a changing environment

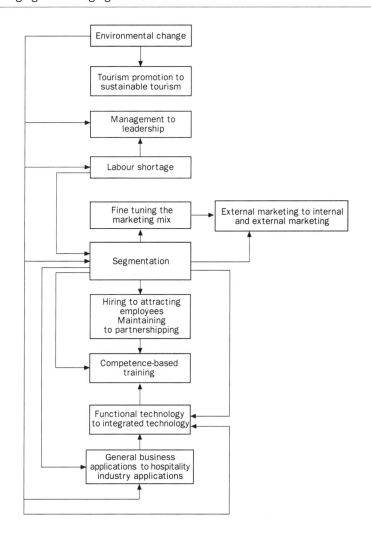

John T. Bowen
*Managing environmental
change: insights from
researchers and practitioners*

18 O'Halloran, P.M., "Management training theories: tools for hospitality managers and trainers", Vol. 9 No. 1, 1991, pp. 67-84.

19 Crafts, D., "Managers' perceptions of alcohol service training programs", Vol. 11 No. 1, 1993, pp. 1-10.

20 Lynn, C., "Training methods utilized by independent restaurant managers", Vol. 12 No. 1, 1994, pp. 51-8.

21 Breiter, D., Cargill, C. and Fried-Kline, S., "An industry view of experiential learning", Vol. 13 No. 1, 1995, pp. 75-80.

22 O'Halloran, R.M., "A case study in crisis management: Le Petit Gourmet catering", Vol. 13 No. 2, 1995, pp. 5-14.

23 Fisher, W.P., "Food service management: a case study in adaptation", Vol. 13 No. 2, 1995, pp. 1-4.

24 Kent, W.E., "Vanguard management: an emerging new paradigm", Vol. 10 No. 1, 1992, pp. 53-64.

25 Cichy, R.F., Sciarini, M.P., Cook, C.L. and Patton, M., "Leadership in the lodging and non-commercial food service industries", Vol. 9 No. 1, 1991, pp. 1-10.

26 Goll, G.E., "Management misperceptions: an obstacle to motivation", Vol. 7 No. 1, 1989, pp. 85-91.

27 Meyer, R.A. and Schroeder, J.J., "Rewarding non-productivity in the hospitality industry", Vol. 7 No. 1, 1989, pp. 1-12.

28 George, R.T., "Hospitality managers as care-takers and change agents: a reconceptualiza-tion of the position", Vol. 7 No. 1, 1989, pp. 13-22.

29 Lundberg, C.C., "Ideologies about work: comparing hospitality and business students and managers", Vol. 10 No. 1, 1992, pp. 75-82.

30 Cichy, R.F., Aoki, T., Patton, M.E. and Scia-rini, M.P., "The five foundations of leadership in Japan's lodging industry", Vol. 10 No. 2, 1992, pp. 65-78.

31 Ralston, C.E., "Manager-customer relation-ship in food service commissary operations", Vol. 11 No. 2, 1993, pp. 61-72.

32 Eade, V.H. and Jonak, M.A., "Drugs in the workplace: a manager's guide", Vol. 9 No. 2, 1991, pp. 7-14.

33 Eade, V.H., "Drug abuse in the hospitality industry", Vol. 11 No. 2, 1993, pp. 81-6.

34 Silfies, P.J. and Demicco, F.J., "Impact of substance abuse: human resource strategies for the hospitality industry", Vol. 1 No. 2, 1992, p. 79.

35 Ghiselli, R. and Ismail, J.A., "Gauging employee theft and other unacceptable behav-iors in food service operations", Vol. 13 No. 2, 1995, pp. 15-24.

36 Ladki, S.M., "Wellness and obesity: implica-tions for health care costs among restaurant managers", Vol. 12 No. 1, 1994, p. 81.

37 Chandrasekar, V. and Cichy, R.F., "A model for costing absenteeism in hotels", Vol. 8 No. 2, 1990, pp. 49-66.

38 Gregg, J.B. and Johnson, P.M., "Perceptions of discrimination among women as managers in hospitality organizations", Vol. 8 No. 1., 1990, pp. 10-23.

39 Brownell, J., "Women hospitality managers: perceptions of gender-related career chal-lenges", Vol. 11 No. 2, 1993, pp. 19-32.

40 Schmidgall, R.S., "Hotel managers' responses to ethical dilemmas", Vol. 10 No. 1, 1992, pp. 11-18.

41 Nicholls, J.A.F. and Roslow, S., "Segmenting the hotel market", Vol. 7 No. 1, 1989, pp. 39-47.

42 Dickinson, R.H., "'Fun ship's marketing philosophy", Vol. 13 No. 1, 1995, pp. 1-6.

43 Pederson, E.B., "Future seniors: is the hospi-tality industry ready for them?", Vol. 10 No. 2, 1992, pp. 1-8.

44 Pederson, B. and DeMicco, F.J., "Restaurant dining strategies: attracting nutrition con-scious future seniors", Vol. 11 No. 2, 1993, pp. 7-18.

45 Harris, K.J. and West, J.J., "Senior savvy: mature diners' restaurant service expecta-tions", Vol. 13 No. 2, 1995, pp. 35-44.

46 Gustin, M.E. and Weaver, P.A., "The mature market: underlying dimensions and group differences of a potential market for the hotel industry", Vol. 11 No. 2, 1993, pp. 49-60.

47 Pederson, B., "Future seniors and the travel industry", Vol. 12 No. 2, 1994, pp. 59-70.

48 Evans, M. and Murrmann, S.K., "Personal care amenities: are they important attributes in the selection of hotels?", Vol. 7 No. 2, 1989, pp. 19-25.

49 Kapoor, S., "Young adults' interest in nutri-tious fast foods", Vol. 7 No. 1, 1989, pp. 31-8.

50 Cai, L. and Ninemeier, J.D., "Food service styles in Chinese hotels: tradition and tourism pressures merge", Vol. 11 No. 2, 1993, pp. 33-40.

51 Nusbaum, E.F., "GENIAL design: a system for improving satisfaction with hospitality design", Vol. 7 No. 1, 1989, pp. 48-54.

52 Morcos, S.H., Tak, J. and Gregoire, M.B., "Customer perceptions of drive-thru ser-vice", Vol. 10 No. 2, 1992, pp. 17-24.

53 Strick, S.K., Montgomery, R.J. and Gant, C., "Restaurant service for the '90s", Vol. 10 No. 2, 1992, pp. 43-8.

54 Holland, M.A. and McCool, A.C., "Cross-culture cuisine: long-term trend or short lived fad", Vol. 12 No. 1, 1994, pp. 17-30.

55 Dienhart, J.R. and Lefever, M.M., "Restaurant marquees: a help or hindrance?" Vol. 7 No. 2, 1989, pp. 77-83.

56 Barrows, C.W., Lattuca, F.P. and Bosselman, R.H., "Influence of restaurant reviews upon consumers", Vol. 7 No. 2, 1989, p. 84.

57 Strate, L.D., "Advertising legalized gambling: a later bloomer under the First Amendment", Vol. 11 No. 1, 1993, pp. 41-56.

58 Smith, K., Gregory, S. and Gould, S. "Place-ment for profit: menu item arrangement on customer-activited computer screens", Vol. 13 No. 2, 1995, pp. 25-34.

59 Gregg, J.B., "Questionnaire construction", Vol. 7 No. 2, 1989, pp. 45-56.

60 Davidson, T.L., "Primary market research: its role in feasibility studies", Vol. 7 No. 1, 1989, pp. 23-30.

61 Vladimir, A.N., "Marketing lessons for the '90s", Vol. 8 No. 2, 1990, pp. 39-48.

62 Chon, K.S. and Whelihan, W.P., "Changing guest preferences and marketing challenges in the resortindustry", Vol. 10 No. 2, 1992, pp. 9-16.

63 Harrison, D.F., "Systematic analysis of change in restaurant operations", Vol. 7 No. 2, 1989, pp. 57-65.

64 Muller, C. and Woods, R.H., "The real failure rate of restaurants", Vol. 9 No. 2, 1991, pp. 60-5.

65 Parsa, H.G. and Khan, M.A., "Trends in the quick service restaurant industry", Vol. 10 No. 1, 1992, pp. 19-26.

66 Chon, K.S. and Huo, Y.H., "Environment for future conference centers: perceptions of managers", Vol. 11 No. 1, 1993, pp. 25-30.

67 Welsh, D.H.B. and Swerdlow, S., "The hospitality gap: bringing Russia into the 21st Century", Vol. 13 No. 2, 1995, pp. 67-76.

68 Kotschevar, L.H., "Nutrition: whose responsibility?" Vol. 7 No. 2, 1989, pp. 10-18.

69 Ahmed, Z.U. and Krohn, F.B., "Marketing dynamics of a hotel tax: the case of Chautauqua County, New York", Vol. 8 No. 2, 1990, pp. 15-26.

70 Myers, J.L. and Urdang, B.S., "Lender liability: the legal and management effects on the hospitality industry", Vol. 10 No. 2, 1992, pp. 35-42.

71 Jaffe, W.F., Almanza, B.A. and Min, C-H.J., "Solid waste disposal: independent food service practices", Vol. 11 No. 1, 1993, pp. 69-78.

72 Gaston, J.R., "Hey! that's my idea: protection from concept copying", Vol. 12 No. 1, 1994, pp. 9-16.

73 Breiter, D. and Fried-Kline, S., "Benchmarking quality management in hotels", Vol. 13 No. 2, 1995, pp. 45-52.

74 Welsh, D.H.B., "Quality performance in our world: what fast service should really mean", *FIU Hospitality Review,* Vol. 8 No. 1, 1990, pp. 41-6.

75 Vladimir, A.N., "Seabourn cruise line: a case study in achieving quality", Vol. 13 No. 1, 1995, pp. 7-22.

76 Haywood, K.M., "Making and evaluating strategy: learning from the military", Vol. 8 No. 2, 1990, pp. 67-78.

77 Williams, A.G., "So...what's wrong with hospitality education?" Vol. 8 No. 1, 1990, p. 72.

78 O'Halloran, R.M., "Tourism management profiles: implications for tourism education", Vol. 10 No. 1, 1992, p. 83.

79 Chesser, J.W. and Ellis, E.T. "Hospitality administration program administrators view core areas of knowledge", Vol. 13 No. 2, 1995, p. 85.

80 Casado, M.A., "Corporate recruiters and alumni: perceptions of professional courses", Vol. 11 No. 1, 1993, p. 79.

81 Casado, M.A., Vallen, G.K. and Miller, W.E., "Ethical challenges of the industry: are graduates prepared", Vol. 12 No. 1, 1994, pp. 1-8.

82 Kasavana, M.L., "Extending the boundaries of hospitality education", Vol. 10 No. 1, 1992, pp. 65-74.

83 Kasavana, M.L., "Advances in hospitality education: courseware, audiographics, and cyberspace", Vol. 11 No. 2, 1993, p. 87.

84 Breiter, D., "Student achievement of experiential learning objectives", Vol. 11 No. 2, 1993, pp. 41-8.

85 Breiter, D., Cargill, C. and Fried-Kline, S., "An industry view of experiential learning", Vol. 13 No. 1, 1995, pp. 75-80.

86 VanDyke, T. and Montgomery, R.J., "Career fairs: what does the industry want?" Vol. 9 No. 2, 1991, pp. 66-71.

87 Jones, T., Izzolo, A.W. and Christianson, D.J., "Campus recruitment: a four-year program profile", Vol. 11 No. 2, 1993, pp. 73 -80.

88 Altman, L.A. and Brothers, L.R., "Career longevity of hospitality graduates", Vol. 13 No. 2, 1995, pp. 77-84.

89 Tarras, J.M. and Schmidgall, R., "Tip allocation: a compliance study for restaurants", Vol. 7 No. 1, 1989, pp. 78-84.

90 Tarras, J.M., "IRS looks closely at independent contractors", Vol. 11 No. 1, 1993, pp. 11-18.

91 VanLoenen, D. and Holland, J.W., "Payroll taxes and personal liability", Vol. 11 No. 1, 1993, pp. 19-24.

92 Damitio, J.W. and Kagle, A.R., "Controllers' perceptions of the importance of accounting skills to lodging managers", Vol. 9 No. 1, 1991, p. 85.

93 Tavlin, E.M., Moncarz, E. and Dumont, D., "Financial failure in the hospitality industry", Vol. 7 No. 1, 1989, pp. 55-77.

94 Moncarz, E.S., "An examination of stock performance: the three top-performing lodging firms August 1987 – January 1990", Vol. 8 No. 2, 1990, p. 79.

95 Moncarz, E.S., "Leveraged buyouts in the hospitality industry: five years later", Vol. 9 No. 1, 1991, pp. 11-24.

96 Schmidgall, R.S., "Financial planning by contract food service management companies", Vol. 9 No. 2, 1991, pp. 15-22.

97 Schmidgall, R.S., "Financial ratios: perceptions of lodging industry general managers, and financial executives", Vol. 7 No. 2, 1989, pp. 1-9.

98 Moncarz, E.S., "Understanding annual reports, of hospitality firms: Part II", Vol. 7 No. 2, 1989, pp. 26-36.

99 Rymer, T.M., "Growth of US ecotourism and its future in the 1990s", Vol. 10 No. 1, 1992, pp. 1-10.

100 O'Halloran, R.M. "Concessions in National Parks: responsible tourism", Vol. 11 No. 1, 1993, pp. 31-40.

101 Yu, L., "Tourism in the Egyptian Red Sea area: a responsible development approach", Vol. 12 No. 2, 1994, pp. 37-44.

102 O'Halloran, R.M. and Holecek, D.F., "Tourism professionals indicate research needs", Vol. 7 No. 2, 1989, pp. 37-44.

103 Sun, L.H. and Uysal, M., "The role of theme parks in tourism", Vol. 12 No. 1, 1994, pp. 71-80.

104 O'Halloran, R.M. and Holecek, D.F., "Issues for managing tourism information", Vol. 9 No. 2, 1991, pp. 23-35.

105 Milman, A., "Canada as a potential vacation destination for Florida residents", Vol. 12 No. 2, 1994, pp. 13-24.

106 Hobson, J.S.P. and Ko, G., "Intra-regional tourism and challenges facing Hong Kong's hotel industry", Vol. 12 No. 2, 1994, pp. 25-36.

107 Kasavana, M.L., "Hospitality information systems: intuitive, object-oriented, and wireless technology", *FIU Hospitality Review,* Vol. 12 No. 1, pp. 37-50.

108 Howey, R.M. and Savage, D.S., "Information processing: coordination and control in large hotels", *FIU Hospitality Review,* Vol. 13 No. 1, 1995, pp. 51-62.

109 Ford, L., Ford, R.C. and LeBruto, S.M., "Is your hotel MISsing technology?", *FIU Hospitality Review,* Vol. 13 No. 2, 1995, pp. 53-66.

110 Collins, G., "Selecting POS systems for table service restaurants", *FIU Hospitality Review,* Vol. 9 No. 2, 1991, pp. 36-51.

111 Jensen, G.L., "Outsourcing information services in the hospitality industry", *FIU Hospitality Review,* Vol. 12 No. 1, 1994, pp. 31-6.

112 Collins, G., "Information technology trends: impact on hotel corporations", *FIU Hospitality Review,* Vol. 13 No. 1, 1995.

113 Singh, A. and Chon, K.S., "Teleconferencing technology: recent developments and implications for hotel industry", *FIU Hospitality Review,* Vol. 11 No. 2, 1993, pp. 1-6.

Clusters and gaps in hospitality and tourism academic research

Hadyn Ingram
Research Manager (Europe) Worldwide Hospitality and Tourism Trends,
Department of Management Studies, University of Surrey, Guildford, UK

Content-analyses the academic entries in the WHATT-CD International Hospitality and Tourism Research Register using four broad categories – general management issues, hospitality, tourism, and current or "hot" research issues. Identifies clusters of research interest within these categories and identifies "gaps" in the form of relatively unexplored research topic areas.

Introduction

In its initial year of operation, the WHATT-CD Research Register has established a central resource of completed and ongoing research in the hospitality and tourism industries. From the researcher's viewpoint, it is useful to tap into a "one-stop" source of related studies and to have the opportunity to network with like-minded people. This article reviews the origins and content of the Research Register entries and comments on its relevance to the needs of hospitality and tourism researchers. The structure is as follows:
- sources of entries analysed by academic award and institution;
- content analysis of research entries, grouped in four categories;
- comment on gaps and overlaps in research.

Source of entries

In total, there were 820 postgraduate research project entries (727 finished and 92 in progress) on the spring 1995 edition of the CD-ROM, with completion dates ranging from 1976 to 1999. Table I shows the sources of the research entries and that all but 16 per cent were submitted from academic institutions.

The vast majority of entries (84 per cent) emanate from academic institutions and, in this category, 296 projects (43 per cent) are MPhil/PhD level and 175 MSc level projects undertaken by full or part-time research students or academic staff (see Table II).

It is pleasing to note the wide geographical spread of sources, with entries from 209 institutions in the UK, Belgium, Austria, Spain, Sweden, USA, Canada, South Africa and Australia. Most of the institutions submitted small numbers of studies and only 16 contributed entries in double figures.

Content analysis

This article seeks to map the International Research Register entries by content-analysing subject terms. Users of WHATT-CD are able to access and filter the information they seek using the following categories:

- names of researcher or adviser;
- research type, level and status (in progress or finished);
- institution of researcher;
- year begun or completed;
- glossary of subject terms.

Each entry in the Register is classified according to its area of interest using four keywords, and to determine patterns keywords were clustered in intuitively-determined thematic categories as follows:
- general – overall subjects including management subject areas and techniques as well as external issues affecting organizations;
- hospitality – hotel or catering-related entries;
- tourism – entries associated with general tourism issues or destinations;
- "hot" issues – current areas of interest and concern.

Each of the four themes is examined and exemplified with reference to ongoing and completed projects.

General issues

This is a large theme area comprising items of broad interest which transcend industry sectors or single disciplines and may be further divided into three sub-themes:
1 operations – general management, operations management, facilities management;
2 support services – legal, financial, marketing and research support;
3 people – careers, education, training and human resource management.

A common feature here is the emphasis placed on planning and strategy. One example is Tracy Jones' 1991 MPhil project at Oxford Brookes University, UK, which recognizes that hotel managers need an effective information system to assist in decision making. She concludes that information needs should be more consciously determined using critical success factors and measures. Another important measure of organizational success is cash flow which is being studied by Eugene Gouws of the University of Pretoria in South Africa. His research aim is to identify the

Hadyn Ingram
*Clusters and gaps in
hospitality and tourism
academic research*

Table I

Sources of research register entries

Category	Number	Percentage
Academic	689	84
Associations	23	3
Government	41	5
Industry	67	8
Total	820	100

Table II

Postgraduate level academic research in academic institutions

Award	Number	Percentage
MA	30	4
MBA	14	2
MPhil	22	3
MSc	175	25
PhD	296	43
Other	152	22
Total *	689	100

Note* total excludes post-doctoral studies and non award-bearing work

determinants of cash flow in a recreational setting as they relate to decision-making processes.

It is perhaps inevitable that the "general" area should be the largest thematic grouping in the Research Register and the one that demonstrates the widest scope. Each of the three sub-themes (operations, support services and people) reflect an interest in "managing effectively" and are fertile areas for academic research. They also recognize the importance of sociocultural and behavioural factors in managing organizations. This is manifest in a "softer" approach to systems and strategy characterized by flexibility and a greater awareness of the importance of people. The role of management is still seen as a pivotal one, but its focus is regarded by researchers as more facilitative than directive.

Hospitality

The hospitality category includes items relating to hotels, catering and other sectors such as leisure and gambling and one issue which cuts across all hospitality industry sectors is information technology (IT). The far-reaching implications of IT are exemplified by Marian Whitaker's PhD research project which suggests that there is nothing inevitable about the impact of new technology on employment. She observes that, when low thresholds of trust occur, employees' reactions to new technology are likely to be negative. Allen Freedman of Nova University, New York, considers the business ethics of hospitality managers and students in his DBA research. His findings suggest that while personal commitment scores were similar for male and female managers, female managers achieve higher overall scores in their commitment to the welfare of others, whereas their male counterparts tend to display greater commitment to profit maximization.

The entries relating to "gastronomy" make interesting reading as this is an area where postgraduate research could be of benefit to industry and customer alike. There is much yet to be discovered about the sociocultural and sensory components of human taste and two PhD research projects from Bournemouth University, UK, and Cornell University, USA, respectively, tackle this topic in different ways. The first by Louise Black-well investigates the role of the senses, particularly smell, in guiding food choice, selection and acceptability. Jennifer Crouch's research into public beer selection and consumption in the USA recognizes that social boundary-setting, as well as taste, are determinants of beer choice. Both projects suggest that sensory and environmental factors can be manipulated by managers to enhance sales or to attract selected customer segments. Greater sophistication in food and drink marketing may be regarded as exploitative, but can also assist in the increasingly complex task of mapping changing consumer tastes.

Most of the entries in this theme area relate to the leisure and hotel sectors while food and catering entries show a marketing or science focus and rarely relate to operational or service issues. In general, the research entries reflect a widely-perceived need for a clearer understanding of the nature of hospitality and for increased levels of professionalism in the future. It is notable that many of the research projects seek to map emerging trends and study global strategies rather than address the problems of individual hospitality units.

Tourism

Tourism entries include items of general tourism interest and those which concern specific tourism destinations. General items span leisure, tranport and the future of the tourism industry. Both developed and developing nations seem to realize the benefits of tourism in earning foreign currency and stimulating local economies. Hard economic exigencies contrast with softer but equally valid concerns about the consequences for the natural environment. Desirable tourism is more often described as "sustainable"; an adjective which seems to incorporate both hard and soft ideals. Jane Rasbash's MSc research studies "green" tourism in Scotland and concludes (in common with many other tourism studies) that cohesive, strategic planning is a requirement for the future. The largest single area of research study is the European Community, but most tourism projects relate to destinations where tourism is, as yet, not fully developed such as Africa, South-east Asia and South America.

One topic which transcends international boundaries is the classification and grading of hotels by public and private organizations. There are currently just four projects in this category which relate to Scotland, Europe and Africa respectively. Susan Kunkel's MA project at the California State University encapsulates the problems inherent in producing an accurate and digestible representation of a country or its accommodation. Tourist or accommodation guidebooks need to reconcile the divergent needs of the intended reader, the service provider and the competitive commercial environment.

As tourism grows in economic importance, it is more often the focus of academic research. Research in this area can assist in benchmarking good practice and detecting emerging trends in demand and tourism provision. The projects show that, although world tourism is growing, established tourism destinations are keen to maintain market share while newer destinations wish to develop their product. Destination development is seen as a long-term commitment in which environmental issues must play a part in the overall tourism strategy. Perhaps future research should seek to determine clearer links between micro and macro tourism issues; that is, to explain local tourism success with reference to tourism theory.

"Hot" issues

"Hot" issues are those which are regarded by society as increasingly important and which are the subject of lively debate in the wider community. The projects reviewed here have been grouped into five sub-themes as shown in Table III. In the face of more intense marketplace rivalry, it is reassuring to note that nearly half the ongoing research relates to customers, service and quality. Despite the mega-growth predictions for tourism and hospitality, most firms realize that a market-oriented approach offers the best opportunity for survival and growth in the future. It seems that this perspective is shared by academic researchers, too.

Most of the entries on "healthy eating" emanate from North America and they reflect concerns about the high level of fat and cholesterol intake in the North American diet. Ewan Gillon from Queen Margaret College in Edinburgh also addresses this issue and specifically the differences in the eating habits of men and women. His findings highlight relatively high levels of awareness of the link between food diet and health among women but also highlight the difficulties associated with managing dietary change.

Issues of current interest offer the academic researcher the opportunity to explore areas which need greater exposure and to provide an interpretation on their future importance to the industry. Such issues only remain "hot" if they have the potential to influence change in the medium to long term and to affect the way in which organizations respond to them. The judicious selection of research topic can be of benefit both to the career of the researcher and to the development of appropriate organizational approaches to emerging problems.

Gaps and overlaps in research

In the first annual review of hospitality and tourism trends (*International Journal of Contemporary Hospitality Management*, Vol.7 No. 7, 1995, pp. iv-vi), Julian Demetriadi comments on some perceived research "gaps". He suggests that some sectors have been ignored such as school meals, camping, forces catering, ferries and pubs. Despite the size and popularity of the uniquely British pub sector there are currently few research projects in

Table III
"Hot" issues in the International Research Register entries

Sub-themes	Areas of focus
Changing patterns	Trends, health and safety, "green issues", disability, health eating
Customers	Consumer behaviour, customer needs
Agencies	Consultants, government agencies, professional trade organizations
Information technology	Technological impacts, management information systems, software advances
Service/quality	Service quality, quality standards, service delivery, total quality management

Hadyn Ingram
*Clusters and gaps in
hospitality and tourism
academic research*

this field. Alison Dingle's MSc research focuses on the British pub as a unique tourism opportunity with the potential to supply informal, value-for-money meals to an expanding dining out market. From the viewpoint of the drinks suppliers, a research project undertaken by the Brewers and Licensed Retailers Association predictably concludes that the reduction in beer duty is both socially and economically desirable.

In general, it is the non-commercial domain that is most under-represented in the Register. Some examples are the hospital and institutional sectors which play so great a part in improving the quality of life of people and communities. Paradoxically, structural changes in these neglected sectors may make research even more important, but the choice of research project rests mostly in the hands of independent researchers. It seems inevitable that there will continue to be both gaps and overlaps in research focus, perhaps because of the different perceptions and priorities of practitioners and academics. Practitioners might be expected to be concerned about seemingly irreconcilable issues that nevertheless affect operations and strategy. Such concerns include the problems of ensuring consistent quality despite staff turnover, shortages of key trained employees and pressures for efficiency improvements. Another key issue is the use of systems and information technology in decision making and operations. In addition, managers in the hospitality and tourism industries may be concerned with the identification of potential markets or products for the future. Other issues include the implications of privatization, the changing role of women in the industry and the continuous growth of short-break holidays.

Overlaps exist in some of the tourism destination projects. Although the projects refer to different geographical destinations, the research findings are often similar in nature. The projects emphasize that tourism is an important potential source of revenue and foreign earnings for many emerging countries and it is understandable than postgraduate students would wish to relate their dissertations to familiar contexts. However, many of the projects have limited application beyond the context of the study.

Concluding comment

The body of research as reflected by entries in the International Research Register seems to be shaped in two major ways. First the

content of entries perhaps inevitably reflects the personal interests of the researcher rather than the needs of others such as those of industry or the wider academic community. In practice, subject choice is also affected by the availability and amount of information. Second, a comprehensive but voluntary Register relies on awareness and goodwill which will grow over time. Many vocational institutions of higher education have postgraduate students who need to research important issues in order to make original contributions to a field of study. Those who undertake postgraduate research, unless they are mature students, often have limited experience of the specific problems of the hospitality and tourism industries. While researchers need to take an objective view, they also need the co-operation of organizations to conduct and to shape primary research. These researchers have the necessary time, intellect and resources to make this possible, but need opportunities to conduct primary research in an industrial context. In summary, bridges need to be built to span the perceived rift between industry and academia because there is much to be gained and little to be lost from greater interchange.

Sectorial gaps may be inevitable, not least because of the long-term nature of postgraduate research. "Hot" issues may disappoint by cooling over time, and research can help in this regard. Primary research, informed analysis and interpretative comment can assist in mapping patterns in a mass of complex interrelated phenomena by differentiating the long-term trend from the short-term fad. If interpreted intelligently, research can also help to make sense of confusion and to predict likely events in the future.

In the longer term, research methodologies may provide the key to learning in the future. The academic community is beginning to come to terms with qualitative methodologies as valid techniques with which to map the inherent richness of hospitality and tourism activities. More experimentation and interchange is needed to develop methodologies through which research may be made more accessible and credible to the world at large. In the search for greater professionalism in hospitality and tourism, an expanded and truly international version of the WHATT-CD Research Register is a valuable resource.

A summary of the main themes and sub-themes is presented in Figure 1.

Hadyn Ingram
*Clusters and gaps in
hospitality and tourism
academic research*

Figure 1
Summary of the main themes and sub-themes

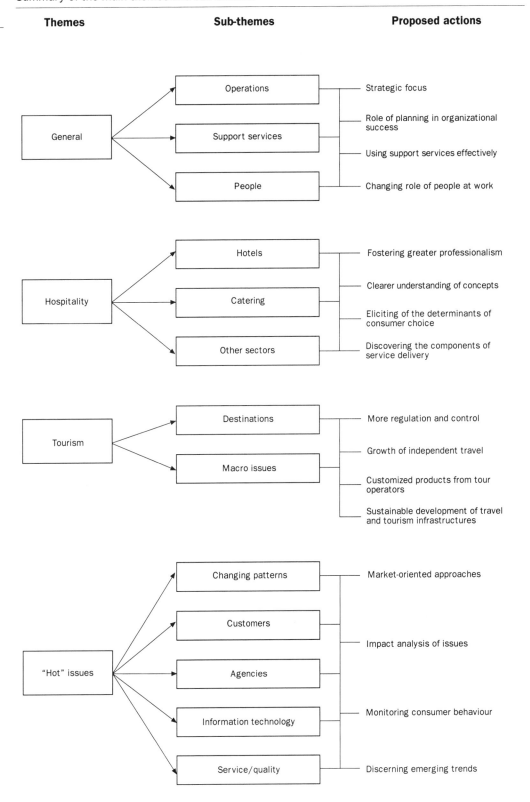

Author and title index to volume 8, 1996

The 1997 Volume of International Journal of Contemporary Hospitality Management

Maximizing value for money

Recent advances in technology have allowed MCB to structure the journals it publishes in such a way that subscribers can ensure that they can exploit each journal's content to the full. Accordingly in 1997 the *International Journal of Contemporary Hospitality Management* will be published in three formats ensuring that the journal's content:

- is available to a number of potential users concurrently
- can be effectively browsed for current awareness and
- can be efficiently searched for information retrieval.

1. Print

The printed journal issue remains the easiest way to keep in touch with new developments in the subject area covered by *International Journal of Contemporary Hospitality Management*. Because so many people have little time to browse through individual issues the *International Journal of Contemporary Hospitality Management* will be published with three double and one single issue in 1997. This means that a subscriber need only browse through four issues while still having access to as many articles as in previous volumes.

2. CD-ROM archive

It is an unfortunate fact that many journal issues are only fully exploited while they are the current issue. Lack of simple search and retrieval mechanisms combined with an unwieldy format means that back volumes of titles become an under-used asset. The CD-ROM provided with the 1996 volume will have shown subscribers the benefits of having the full text of two volumes and abstracts of previous volumes combined with sophisticated search techniques thus allowing precise information to be retrieved.

In 1997 this CD-ROM will be augmented not only through the addition of the full text of material published in the 1996 volume but also through the provision of a licence allowing the CD-ROM to be networked to as many workstations as the subscriber wishes. This ensures that the material can be easily searched by users through the convenience of instant access from their place of work.

3. Internet/continuous publishing

The emergence of the Internet as a medium for publication brings significant advantages. MCB has included continuous publishing via the Internet in the 1997 subscription to the *International Journal of Contemporary Hospitality Management* and this allows the journal's content to be updated on a much more frequent basis than the print version. The Internet site will be updated on a monthly basis ensuring that individuals with a particular interest in the subject covered can be kept informed of the very latest developments. Articles may be viewed either on an "issue" basis or retrieved by author, subject or posting date.

As with the CD-ROM the Internet version of the journal will be accessible from multiple points within a subscribing organization. Any user with the domain name of the subscribing organization as part of their Internet address will be able to access the material published electronically by the *International Journal of Contemporary Hospitality Management*. The journal's archive will also be available via the Internet and searchable on the same dimensions as the CD-ROM.

Subscribers who cannot use electronic enhancements

It is recognized that there are some subscribers who cannot exploit electronic media for journal article delivery. Such subscribers can also enjoy MCB's policy of multiple access through the provision of multiple copies of the printed journal issues. The maximum number of copies available to a single subscriber will be three. All copies will be despatched to the subscriber and should be forwarded internally to further users within the subscribing institution or organization.

The 1997 volume of the *International Journal of Contemporary Hospitality Management* will continue to provide its readers with information at the leading edge of the subject. The multiple access model which will be provided for the journal will ensure that the maximum number of individuals within a subscribing organization can benefit from the material published. Thus the more the journal is used the better value the subscription represents.